JAMES DYER

Discovering Archaeology in England and Wales

SHIRE PUBLICATIONS LTD

British Library Cataloguing in Publication Data: Dyer, James, 1934-. Discovering archaeology in England and Wales. – 6th ed. – (Discovering; 46). 1. England – Antiquities. 2. Wales – Antiquities. 3. Great Britain – History – To 1066. I. Title. 936.2. ISBN 0 7478 0333 1.

Cover: *The rescue excavation of a double child burial from a neolithic ring ditch at Bury Farm, Goldington, on the outskirts of Bedford in 1987. (Photograph: Bedfordshire County Archaeology Service.)*

Published in 1997 by Shire Publications Ltd, Cromwell House, Church Street, Princes Risborough, Buckinghamshire HP27 9AA, UK. Copyright © 1969, 1985 and 1997 by James Dyer. First published 1969, reprinted 1969. Second edition 1971. Third edition 1973. Fourth edition 1976, reprinted 1980. Fifth edition 1985, reprinted 1990. Sixth edition, rewritten and expanded, 1997. Number 46 in the Discovering series. ISBN 0 7478 0333 1.
James Dyer is hereby identified as the author of this work in accordance with section 77 of the Copyright, Designs and Patents Act, 1988.

Printed in Great Britain by CIT Printing Services, Press Buildings, Merlins Bridge, Haverfordwest, Pembrokeshire SA61 1XF.

Contents

Introduction

In his splendidly down to earth book *Invitation to Archaeology* (Blackwell, 1985) Professor Philip Rahtz poses the basic question 'Why do people do archaeology?'. His answer is simple: 'It is done for enjoyment, and because it is actually important.' That is why I first wrote this book in 1969, and now, after rewriting much of it, I feel that its message is as strong as ever. Taking part in my first excavation at Dorchester-on-Thames in 1949 was the beginning of a great historical adventure. It led to an addiction that has occupied most of my free time ever since. It also introduced me to a strict new discipline. I soon learnt that excavation had to be meticulous and honest, carried out with the skill of a surgeon. If it was not done properly the first time, there was no second chance. An excavation was final; it could not be repeated; if missed, evidence was lost for ever. Every scrap of evidence gained must be added to our rapidly growing knowledge of the past.

The puzzle of the past holds a fascination for many people, be it just a passing curiosity or a burning desire to get as close to the truth as possible. Like Philip Rahtz, I think this is important. I find it most disappointing that the National Curriculum, foisted upon Britain's schools, allows little room for the study of the earliest, and for many people the most fascinating, part of the nation's story. I now offer a new edition of this little book as an attempt to counter this sad omission. I hope that it will help students of all ages to take their first steps to understanding the work of archaeologists and the story that they are uncovering.

In *Discovering Archaeology in England and Wales* I have attempted to describe some of the most common scientific methods now being used to elucidate the past, followed by an outline of the history of Britain from the the first appearance of *Homo sapiens* a quarter of a million years ago to the arrival of the Normans in 1066. I believe that it will also prove useful for visitors to museums, ancient monuments and excavations, who require some further explanation of what they are observing. An unfamiliar word or phrase in a museum label or guide book may often conceal much fascinating information: reference to the index at the end of this book should lead the reader to this information. The main explanation of an archaeological term is indicated in heavy type.

I have to thank a number of people who have assisted in the preparation of all editions of this book, and in particular: F. K. Annable; Dr Ilid Anthony; Evelyn Baker; Kevan Fadden; Ann Hagen; Anthony J. Hales; Professor W. H. Manning; Dr Joshua

Pollard; Nicholas Thomas; and Dr John Wymer.

Photographs are acknowledged as follows: Bedfordshire County Archaeology Service, cover, 5, 10, 54; Cambridge University Collection, copyright reserved, 6, 68; Kevan Fadden, 41; J. E. Hancock, 16, 35; Cadbury Lamb, 69, 76; W. H. Manning, 67, 71, 73; Francis Pryor, 12, 43; H. Senogles, 27; Nicholas Thomas, 9; William Wadsworth, 75; Wiltshire Archaeological and Natural History Society (Devizes Museum), 38, 46, 57, 62. The remaining photographs and drawings are by the author. Figures 13, 23, 37, 49, 61 and 74 were taken in Bedford Museum.

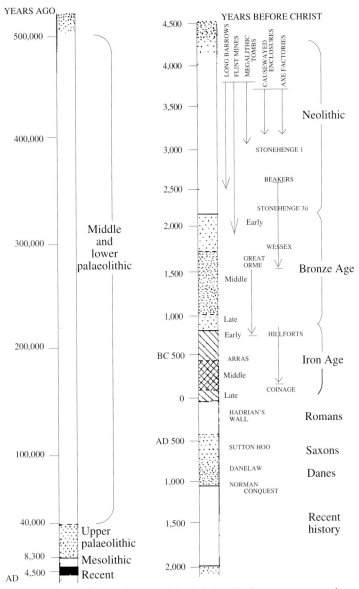

Time chart. The black area of the left-hand column represents the period covered by the whole of the column on the right.

6

1
What is archaeology?

Archaeology is the study of how people lived in the past, based on the things they left behind them, which are often known as their material culture. Archaeologists have the difficult task of trying to explain this material culture in human terms. Many years ago the distinguished archaeologist Sir Mortimer Wheeler reminded us that he was not digging up things but people, something frequently forgotten by writers of the thousands of technical reports that have appeared over the years.

The archaeologist, then, uses the everyday things made by earlier people to reconstruct their daily lives: their pots and tools, their weapons and jewellery. These take the place of the documents and records used by the historian to reconstruct life in historic times, although the methods of the archaeologist can be used to solve historical problems too. Medieval documents do not often give much information about the home life of a twelfth-century peasant, for example, though the excavation of his village might tell us a great deal.

Often the archaeologist is dealing with the earliest periods of human existence, and his work is linked with that of the geologist and the anthropologist. As man developed, so the work of the archaeologist and the prehistorian go hand in hand. Indeed all prehistorians are basically archaeologists. Prehistory is the time framework into which archaeologists fit the remains of the earliest of the people they are studying before the invasion of the Emperor Claudius in AD 43. The study of Roman and Saxon Britain will also come within the scope of the archaeologists, although here some documents exist; but so great are the gaps that archaeology is called upon to fill them. As we approach more recent times so the calls on the archaeologist become fewer, but medieval and industrial archaeology are legitimate studies which supplement the work of the historians, the latter dealing with buildings and engineering works constructed during the industrial revolution. Today archaeologists in Britain are identifying and recording the surviving remains of the military constructions of the First and Second World Wars, before they have all vanished.

Many people think of archaeology as excavation. The first excavations we know about were made by an Assyrian princess, Ennigaldi-Nanna, more than five hundred years before Christ. The princess collected her finds into one of the first museums, at Ur of the Chaldees in present-day Iraq. It was excavated by Sir Leonard Woolley in the 1920s. The Greeks and Romans visited and col-

1. William Stukeley's drawing of Ravensburgh Castle hillfort near Hexton in Hertfordshire in 1724. Today the site is covered with trees.

lected antiquities but, as far as we are aware, did not excavate. Indeed excavation has developed only in the last three hundred years.

Records of archaeological sites first began to appear during the sixteenth, seventeenth and eighteenth centuries, with the work of people like John Leland (*c*.1503-52), whose *Itinerary* was published in 1710 long after his death; Sir Thomas Browne (1605-82), the Norfolk physician whose *Urne Burial* is possibly the earliest excavation report; John Aubrey (1627-97), who recorded archaeological sites he found around Britain in his only recently published *Monumenta Britannica*; and William Stukeley (1687-1765), who began a fashionable interest in antiquities and produced, amongst other works, his profusely illustrated *Itinerarium Curiosum* (1724), and his detailed studies of Stonehenge and Avebury. Stukeley set out on his travels 'to oblige the curious in the Antiquities of Britain' and to compile 'an account of places and things for inspection, not compiled from others' labours, or travels in one's study'. These were noble sentiments and had much to recommend them. Unfortunately, in trying to link the places he visited with what he knew of early history, which was entirely gleaned from the Bible and classical writings, he allowed his imagination to run riot, and he soon invalidated his careful observations with elaborate theories of Druids and snake worship. It is the genius of his fertile

2. Thomas Bateman digging into Taylor's Low barrow near Wetton (Staffordshire) in 1845.

imagination which has attributed the indestructible stories of Druids to almost all our stone circles, these 'rude stone monuments' as our ancestors called them (figure 1).

During the eighteenth century the interest in antiquities grew and it is not surprising that before long men stopped theorising about monuments and turned to digging them up. In 1730 Cromwell Mortimer, an 'impertinent, assuming, empiric physician', was digging Saxon burial mounds at Chartham in east Kent. For the next two hundred years the interest in excavation increased, multiplied and mushroomed. Such pioneers as Bryan Faussett in Kent, William Cunnington and Sir Richard Colt Hoare in Wessex, Thomas and William Bateman in Derbyshire, Charles Warne in Dorset, Canon Greenwell and J. R. Mortimer in Yorkshire and the Reverend W. G. Lukis and W. C. Borlase in Cornwall worked with methods which, with hindsight, we tend to deplore today (figure 2). Without their discoveries, however, our museums would have lacked the sort of objects which made it possible for the Danish archaeologist Christian Thomsen, working in the Old Nordic Museum in Copenhagen, to arrange for the first time his exhibits in separate rooms devoted to objects of stone, bronze and iron. This established what became known as the Three Age system of classification. It was left to his successor, J. J. A. Worsaae, to prove by excavation that objects of the stone age were older than those of the bronze age, and all older than the iron age. It was Worsaae's book *Primeval Antiquities of Denmark* (published in England in 1849) that made the Three Age system known to British archaeologists, although it was not adopted at the British Museum until 1866, and then rather reluctantly.

An Englishman, John Lubbock (who later became Lord Avebury), took the Three Age system a step further when in his book *Prehistoric Times*, published in 1865, he introduced a fourth age, or at least a modification of the first. This resulted in the palaeolithic or old stone age, neolithic or new stone age, bronze age and iron age. It is this general pattern, with one further modification – the introduction of a mesolithic or middle stone age by Westropp in 1866 – that has lasted as a yardstick until the present day. However, with more accurate dating methods, archaeologists tend to replace these approximate 'period' names with actual dates whenever possible.

Stimulated by the excavation of classical sites like Pompeii and Herculaneum, English gentlemen returning home from the Grand Tour began to dig for antiquities in the English and Welsh countryside. Most of the excavations of the eighteenth and nineteenth centuries were little more than treasure hunts. It was invariably burial mounds that attracted most attention. A hole was dug from the summit down to the centre in the hope of finding a burial deposit, preferably accompanied by urns and equipment which could be displayed as barrow-digging trophies. These 'excavations' were carried out at great speed, the Reverend Bryan Faussett probably holding the record with thirty-one barrows opened in one day in 1771! Today a month would be a reasonable average for the excavation of one such barrow.

Between 1800 and 1810 more than 450 burial mounds were opened by William Cunnington of Heytesbury, who, in a very rudimentary way, first appreciated the principles of modern excavation. He saw digging as a means of answering questions, not simply as a way of obtaining objects for his collection. He submitted soil and bone samples for analysis and insisted on the labelling of all the objects he found. His work was published by his patron, Sir Richard Colt Hoare.

In the last two decades of the nineteenth century there was a great change in excavation methods. This was brought about by one man, Augustus Lane Fox, who in 1880 changed his name to Pitt-Rivers on inheriting a vast estate on Cranborne Chase in Dorset. Trained as a soldier, General Pitt-Rivers demanded the highest standards from his workmen. He insisted on the total excavation of a site, making plans and sections of what he observed, and providing drawings and descriptions of all the objects he found. He observed that all excavation is destructive and that records of the exercise should be so complete that it would be possible to reconstruct everything exactly as it was found. So thoroughly did he observe this dictum that sixty years later Professor C. F. C. Hawkes was able to do just this from the General's published excavation accounts.

Pitt-Rivers's methods were carried on into the twentieth century by his assistant, Harold St George Gray, who excavated the Glastonbury and Meare lake settlements, Maumbury Rings and Avebury. In the 1930s another military man, the flamboyant Mortimer Wheeler, developed a series of techniques for large excavations which included box-shaped trenches known as grid systems, detailed observations of cross-sections and three-dimensional recording (figure 3). In Britain Wheeler's methods dominated for the next thirty years, although they were often unsuitable in less skilful hands and on small sites where important details might be lost beneath baulks of undug earth. This was particularly true on prehistoric sites where slight changes in soil colour or texture were often the only indication of the presence of former postholes or foundation trenches that might easily be missed.

It was the work of continental archaeologists like the German Gerhard Bersu (interned in the Isle of Man in 1940), A. E. van

3. The grid system of excavation, developed by Mortimer Wheeler, in use at Conderton Camp (Worcestershire) in 1958.

4. A large site at Abingdon (Oxfordshire) stripped by the area excavation method. In the centre is the footing trench of a circular hut. The semicircular trench in the foreground held a fence to shelter the hut door.

Giffen in the Netherlands, Gudmund Hatt and Poul Norlund in Denmark which demonstrated the efficacy of large-scale open-area excavation in which a detailed three-dimensional study was made in plan and depth of every layer of soil excavated, and from which every possible scrap of information was extracted. Excavations of this type were pioneered in Britain by Brian Hope-Taylor at Yeavering (Northumberland), in the 1950s and by Martin Biddle at Winchester, Philip Rahtz at Cheddar and Leslie Alcock at South Cadbury in the 1960s (figure 4). At the same time a host of other disciplines was being called upon to help interpret the material found, ranging through anthropology, physics, biology, geology and climatology. With the proliferation of scientific techniques, especially in the field of dating sites and objects, these disciplines made it possible to obtain a vast range of details undreamed of half a century before.

During the mid twentieth century extensive building development in urban areas and the construction of a vast network of motorways caused a tremendous acceleration in the destruction of archaeological remains, which resulted in a crisis for archaeologists. Building motorways also had an often forgotten domino effect in destroying the landscape: the massive quarries opened up to obtain minerals for roadmaking uncovered huge expanses of archaeological deposits which required an altogether broader approach. Where excavations had previously been largely funded by universities, museums, archaeological societies and private individuals, it was now necessary for the state to contribute more to the financing of emergency excavations. It had had the power to do so, but seldom used it, since the passing of the Ancient Monuments Act of 1931. The result of this excavation explosion became known as **rescue archaeology** and a pressure group called Rescue, founded in 1971, campaigned to raise public awareness of the scale of destruction.

All over Britain archaeological units were set up with funding from local and national government. Often based on county planning departments, the first units appeared in 1973 in Oxford, London and Southampton. Others quickly followed, and for a few halcyon years archaeology 'on the rates' prospered. Each county had its own senior archaeologist, responsible, amongst other things, for setting up a Sites and Monuments Record and vetting planning proposals in sensitive areas. The Manpower Services Commission, a scheme to relieve unemployment in the 1980s, provided a wealth of government-funded (but largely untrained) labour with fixed working hours and wages. A massive excavation programme followed. Volunteer labour from local archaeological societies and the interested general public had for years provided the skilled diggers on British excavations: now there was a growing tension between the local weekend amateurs and the new professionals.

In 1988 government funding came to an abrupt end and a number of units were forced to close down. Others reformed as private contractors, tendering to excavate threatened sites prior to development. In 1990 the Department of the Environment published PPG16 (Planning Policy Guidance Note number 16), which was an advisory note which 'advocated the presumption of preserving important archaeological sites and their settings, and supplied the mechanism by which financial resources for any necessary assessment, evaluation, excavation and analysis could be provided by the developer'. County archaeologists, usually attached to the Planning Office, continued to operate the Sites and Monuments Record, and to vet all planning proposals for possible archaeological conflict. Where the planning proposal was seen as a possible threat to an archaeological site, then it was necessary for the County Archaeologist to assess the situation, including gathering sufficient information, if necessary by prior investigation (**evaluation**), to determine the quality, date and extent of the archaeological deposits. Evaluation often includes historical research, topographical survey, fieldwalking, geophysical survey and trial trenching, and is paid for by the developer. The next stage in the process is for the County Archaeologist to devise or approve the best scheme for the protection or recording (or both) of the archaeology of the site under threat.

This has led to a quite different state of affairs; since the developer pays for the excavation and the subsequent analysis, he is free to choose who does the work. This often has to be done to a rapid timescale and to specific standards, with a tendency further to squeeze out the weekend amateur. This has led to competitive tendering, units bidding against each other for contracts, ranging far and wide rather than staying within their immediate locality, and frequently entailing the loss of crucial local knowledge that contributes so much to the understanding of archaeology. There can be no doubt of the dangers inherent in putting the national heritage out to the lowest bidder; this can also militate against public involvement and enjoyment in archaeology.

A new breed of archaeologist has appeared as a result of this development: the archaeological consultant, who advises the developer and sometimes undertakes the work as well. With the increased involvement of the private sector in funding the recording of the national heritage, government funds are decreasing along with their influence on this type of rescue work. The future of British archaeology looks rather bleak.

2
How the archaeologist works

To most people travelling through the towns, cities and country-side of Britain the archaeology of a prehistoric, Roman and early medieval past is far from evident. Occasionally archaeological remains are obvious, such as the megalithic tombs and stone circles of western and northern Britain, the grassy mounds of earthen barrows and hillforts, or Roman town walls and Saxon churches. However, natural and human processes that transform the landscape have done much to hide and eradicate remains of the past. Chief amongst these are the natural decay of timber and other organic structures and artefacts (figure 5), deliberate levelling, robbing and reuse of remains (for example, the use of bricks from the Roman town of Verulamium, St Albans, for the rebuilding of the Norman abbey), and agricultural activity, particularly centuries of ploughing. Without the benefit of historical records or maps archaeologists must adopt a range of techniques for the discovery, investigation and interpretation of sites.

5. Lifting waterlogged timbers preserved at the base of a Saxon well, Salford Quarry (Bedfordshire).

DISCOVERY AND INVESTIGATION

The most obvious approach to the investigation of an archaeological site is through field survey. By this is meant the systematic study of specific areas of the landscape with the aim of detecting and interpreting surface traces of early settlement or other activities. Where an area of land has not suffered the detrimental effects of ploughing or modern building, features such as field ditches, trackways, houses and settlement enclosures may still survive as upstanding walls or earthworks. Through the production of accurate, measured plans it is possible to understand the form, function and often date of such traces, partly by comparison with excavated sites of similar type. In fortunate situations where one earthwork can clearly be seen to cut or overlie another, a sequence of activity can be worked out without the need for excavation. The value of such field observations has long been appreciated: as early as the eighteenth century William Stukeley noticed how the course of a Roman road cut through a round barrow on Oakley Down, Cranborne Chase, thus establishing the prehistoric date of this and similar barrows.

Where upstanding archaeological remains are absent other techniques must be adopted for the detection of sites. Perhaps the most important of these, or at least the one which has produced the most stunning results, is **aerial photography**. The air photograph reveals sites in three ways:

1. *Shadows.* Slight banks and ditches still visible on the ground will be seen clearly from the air in the early morning or evening by the shadows cast when the sun is at a low angle. At the same time light will be reflected from inclined surfaces.

2. *Soil marks.* Sites that have been levelled by ploughing often leave scatters of different coloured soil across bare ploughed fields: the chalk of a burial mound, for example, standing out clearly against the grey humus of a field. This can be clearly seen from the air, although on the ground the marks are a meaningless jumble.

3. *Cropmarks.* Wherever a ditch or pit has been dug into the ground it will have filled with soil looser than that around it. Cereal and leguminous crops over the disturbance will grow darker and higher because of the greater humic and moisture content (figures 6 and 7). The converse effect occurs when plants grow over buried roads, walls, floors, etc. They become stunted and lighter in colour than the surrounding crop. Cropmarks show up best during a drought or after a few weeks of dry weather and are best photographed in June and early July. Such marks also occur in other crops like potatoes and hay, but these are less responsive. They have even been noticed in a row of mature beech trees growing

16

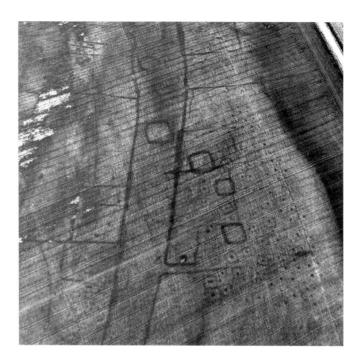

6. An aerial photograph of cropmarks at Burton Fleming in the Yorkshire Wolds. The square enclosures and black dots mark barrow ditches and graves of the Arras culture (see page 85).

7. Corn grows higher and darker over a buried ditch and is sparse and stunted over a wall or hard surface.

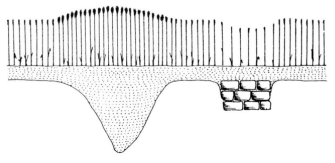

over a filled-in, broad, deep ditch. In areas such as the gravel terraces of the Thames valley aerial photography of previously unknown prehistoric ceremonial monuments and settlement sites, visible only as cropmarks, has transformed our understanding of the use of these early landscapes.

Fieldwalking provides another immensely valuable technique for identifying new sites and discovering something about their function, date and duration of use, without the need for expensive excavation. The technique is very simple and has grown in popularity in the last quarter of the twentieth century. Where a field is ploughed, disturbing buried archaeological deposits, durable artefacts such as sherds of pottery and worked flints will be brought to the surface. By dividing the area to be walked into a grid and systematically collecting all the artefacts lying on the ploughed surface, the density of archaeological remains across the landscape can be reconstructed. Concentrations of pottery or flint tools could mark the location of a settlement, or a general low-density spread of potsherds might represent traces of rubbish mixed with manure and spread over ancient fields, thus indicating the presence of former areas of cultivation. Major campaigns of fieldwalking, for example in the East Anglian Fens and around Stonehenge, have proved hugely successful in identifying new sites.

Sometimes a site is known about, perhaps through fieldwalking, but it is desirable to obtain a plan of it without, or before, having to excavate. In such situations geophysical techniques can be employed, which detect buried features (walls, ditches and pits) by either passing fields of energy through the subsoil or by detecting magnetic variations. The most commonly employed of these techniques is that of **resistivity surveying**, developed as long ago as 1946. A machine is used to detect variations in the electrical resistance of the subsoil by passing a current between two electrodes, the results being recorded on a data logger. Where the slightly more humic and water-retentive fill of a ditch, grave or pit is present the electrical resistance will be low, and conversely a wall or floor would provide a high resistance reading. By taking readings at intervals of a metre or half metre along a preset grid, and then displaying the results as a dot density or contour map, a plan of the buried site can be produced quickly and cheaply. The success of this technique depends on both the weather (it should not be too wet) and the subsoil; it produces particularly good results on chalk and gravel sites.

The **proton magnetometer** is another widely used geophysical device. This works by measuring variations and distortions in the earth's magnetic field. An iron object will obviously produce a strong anomaly, but extremely slight distortion is also caused by buried pits, ditches, ovens, hearths and furnaces. This is because both fire and cultivation have the effect of increasing the weak magnetism of the small amount of iron oxide that is normally present in the soil. By employing the same technique described for resistivity surveying, where readings are taken along a grid, the resulting pattern of magnetic anomalies can illustrate the location of buried features. Unfortunately, metal objects such as fences, overhead cables, and even a watch worn by the archaeologist using the machine, can distort the readings, so it is not a technique that can be used in urban settings. Another version of the magneto-meter, the **fluxgate gradiometer**, can produce continuous readings, allowing very rapid surveys to be made.

Resistivity and magnetometry can detect only features a metre or so below the ground surface and are of little use on urban sites where archaeological deposits may go down several metres. Soil-sounding radar is a new technique which uses radio pulses, the echoes of which reflect changes in soil conditions, producing images of vertical variations in underlying deposits. By taking readings along a series of parallel transects three-dimensional images can be built up. Although still in its infancy, this technique has proved very useful at sites such as medieval York and the Saxon cemetery at Sutton Hoo (Suffolk), at the latter detecting grave pits under upstanding mounds.

Metal detectors are sometimes used in controlled conditions during fieldwalking or on excavations. Their unauthorised use by the public on archaeological sites can cause much damage and, if the site is protected by law, it is illegal. However, responsible users of metal detectors, often members of recognised clubs, do contribute valuable information about unknown sites or stray finds of artefacts by telling local museums or archaeological units about any objects they discover.

Much of the information that archaeologists use to make statements about the past comes from **excavation**. Excavation is a very labour-intensive and costly business and is undertaken only with specific research goals in mind or, more commonly, if a site is threatened by destruction from development. The basic principles of excavation are in theory simple but in practice can be difficult. First, the nature of **stratigraphy** should be considered. Deposits, such as layers, walls, floors or the fills of ditches, pits and graves, have built up over a period of time (whether minutes or millennia). As with geological layers, the lowest will be the earliest and the highest the latest, since the latter must have formed after those beneath it. Excavation proceeds by removing deposits in the re-verse order to which they formed, starting at the top with the latest and proceeding down to the earliest. Where there is no great depth

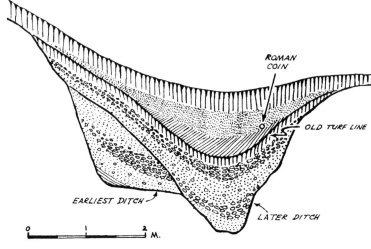

8. An archaeological section drawing of stratification in an iron age ditch at Ravensburgh Castle hillfort (Hertfordshire).

of stratigraphy, as is often the case on plough-damaged sites, but where features are observed to cut through each other, such as a Roman ditch cutting a silted-up bronze age pit, the fills of the latest feature are again excavated first. Vertical **sections** of unexcavated deposits are retained and drawn since these allow an instant visual reading of the sequence of layers and constructional events (figure 8). The choice of where to leave sections is very important and must be done at points where the maximum information about sequences can be gained. A round barrow or large pit, for example, would normally be excavated by removing quadrants, leaving a cross-shaped **baulk** running from the sides to the centre (figure 9).

Excavation is by its nature destructive, and accurate and standard-ised record-keeping is therefore essential. Archaeologists have to be able to make sense of what it is they have dug, and a final understanding of a site will be possible only after excavation is completed, when all aspects of the evidence can be considered. Plans are made of excavated features and layers, usually at a scale of 1:20 and 1:50, and sections are likewise drawn at 1:10. Photo-graphs are taken of the site as a whole throughout the stages of digging, and of particularly important finds and features. A written record is kept. General notes are made in site notebooks and specific descriptions of individual **contexts** (a layer, a fill, a wall, etc) are written on pre-printed sheets. Finds are collected and labelled according to the context from which they came. Samples of soil will be kept for analysis of environmental remains such as charred cereals or small animal bones.

It is rarely possible to excavate a site in total, particularly under rescue conditions when it is threatened by development and resources of time and money are scarce. Decisions therefore have to be taken as to what or how much to dig, and that involves a **sampling** strategy. This may consist of only half-excavating features so that at least they can be seen in section and artefacts can be recovered which will provide evidence of date and function (figure 10). Or, alternatively, a decision might be taken to dig thoroughly only part of a site or levels belonging to a particular period. The purpose of an excavation should be to answer particular questions that the archaeologist considers important, whether these be of dating, function, status, the relationship to other sites, and so on.

An excavation is of little value until a full report of it is published. This should consist of a detailed description of the features revealed, illustrated with plans, section drawings and photographs, along with a considered interpretation. Specialist reports on artefacts, animal and human bones and environmental analyses will also be included. If an excavation continues over a number of years, **interim reports** should be published, since a **final report** is

9. The quadrant system used in excavating a bell-barrow on Snail Down (Wiltshire).

10. *Excavating a drainage ditch surrounding an iron age roundhouse, by removing alternate sections.*

often a long time in production. The choice of where to publish the results depends on the importance of the site. If of only local significance it will probably appear in a county journal such as the *Sussex Archaeological Collections*; if of greater importance then in a recognised national or international journal like the *Proceedings of the Prehistoric Society* or *Archaeologia*. If the report is very extensive then it might be published as a monograph.

INTERPRETING THE SITE

Following on from fieldwork and excavation is the task of interpretation – putting the flesh on the dry bones of the data collected so that a picture of past activities and lives can be built up. There might be several basic questions. How old is a site or artefact? What was its function? How was it made? What was the environment like at the time?

Dating techniques

There are two basic ways to date a site or an artefact: the first by a **relative** dating technique, the second by an **absolute**, or scientific, method. Relative dates are rarely exact and do not usually conform to particular years or fixed periods of time, but they provide a sequence such that it is possible to say that one object or event is earlier or later than another. They are based on stratigraphy, associations and typology. Stratigraphy provides the most obvious means of constructing a sequence, since the succession of layers on a site will always run from the bottom to the latest at the top. By association, any objects found in these layers can then themselves be placed in a chronological order, though it should be remembered that, although an artefact can be no later than the layer in which it was found, it can be earlier. Objects of a known age can then provide a date for items of unknown age if they are found in **association** within a sealed context such as a grave or pit. A flint knife of previously uncertain age found in a grave with a pottery vessel of known later neolithic date will have been contemporary in use if not in manufacture. For example, strangely carved stone balls have been found in many Scottish counties, but until similar stone balls were discovered during the excavation of the neolithic settlement at Skara Brae (Orkney) in the late 1920s their age was unknown.

Typology depends on the assumption that one object evolved out of another. A quill pen, a steel-nibbed dip-pen, a fountain pen and a ballpoint make a typological sequence (figure 11). Usually, but by no means universally, there is a sequence from the technologically simple to the complex; for example, from a stone axe to one of steel, or from a Minoan single-edge bronze razor to a modern stainless steel blade. By placing objects in developmental order a relative sequence of ages is established.

Whilst relative dating provides a working sequence, archaeologists need to know the real ages, in calendar years, of the sites and artefacts they are dealing with. For this a range of absolute dating techniques is available. Probably the most widely used of these is **radiocarbon dating**, first discovered by the American

11. A typological sequence of bronze age axeheads.

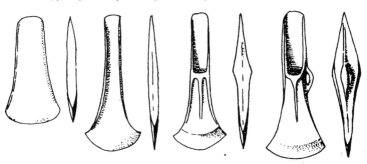

chemist Willard F. Libby in 1949. This technique works by measuring the decay of the radioactive isotope carbon-14. Cosmic rays in the atmosphere form carbon-14, which is then absorbed by all living things through carbon dioxide. When a plant or animal (or a person) dies it ceases to take part in the absorption of this isotope, which then disintegrates through radioactive decay by half every 5730 years. If the remaining radioactive carbon is measured, it is possible to determine how long ago the specimen died. All organic material is suitable for radiocarbon dating – bone, charcoal and wood being most frequently used. With conventional radiocarbon dating a large sample is generally needed, such as a human thigh bone, but a new technique, accelerator mass spectrometry (AMS), which directly detects the number of carbon-14 atoms in a sample relative to those of carbon-13 and carbon-12, allows tiny pieces of organic material to be dated. This has been used in cases where an object is too precious to allow large parts of it to be destroyed, such as in the dating of the Turin Shroud.

The method is not wholly accurate, because of factors such as counting errors and contamination from background cosmic radiation, so all dates are quoted with a standard deviation of plus or minus so many years. It has also been recognised that radiocarbon results are generally 'too young' and become increasingly so with time; they therefore have to be calibrated to convert them to calendar dates. This has been done by taking radiocarbon determinations of tree-rings of a known age and producing a calibration curve from which dates can be corrected. It is standard practice to follow uncorrected radiocarbon dates with the letters *BP* (before present), and dates that have been corrected with *cal BC* or *cal AD*.

Potassium argon dating is somewhat similar to radiocarbon and depends on the breakdown of the potassium isotope K40. This has a half-life of 1,330,000,000 years, thus making the method capable of measuring the greater part of geological time. It can be used only on deposits that are rich in potassium and has been most successful on sites like Olduvai in Tanzania, where the remains of 'Nutcracker Man' (*Zinjanthropus*) have been dated to about 1,750,000 years ago.

Thermoluminescence is a method that can be used to date inorganic material such as pottery and burnt flint. Materials with a crystalline structure contain small amounts of radioactive elements which decay at a known rate, as with carbon-14. These emit radiation, displacing electrons that then become trapped in the crystal lattice of the material. The trapped electrons are released only when the material is heated to over 500°C, during which they emit light known as thermoluminescence. In the case of pottery or the clay lining of a hearth or kiln, the process of electron displacement will begin when it is fired. By measuring the amount of thermoluminescence released when the sample is reheated its age can be established. This method has the advantage of being able to date much older samples than radiocarbon. At Pontnewydd Cave in north Wales early human remains associated with stone tools have been dated to 200,000 years old by this technique.

Archaeomagnetic dating is comparatively little used. It is based on the observation that the magnetic field of the earth is continually changing in direction and intensity. Baked clay structures (which contain iron oxide), such as ovens and kilns, will retain the magnetisation present at the time of firing. It is possible to measure the deviation of the ancient magnetic field from that of today and so to date the object.

Dendrochronology is a simple technique that provides great precision. It allows wood to be dated by using tree-rings as a measurement of time. The annual growth of a tree-ring varies in thickness from year to year depending on the rainfall. Similar thickness variations occur in all trees in a given region, the pattern of broad and thin rings in one tree closely matching the pattern in another. If sections of wood of overlapping age are taken it is possible to correlate the rings and build up a scale of dates stretching back into prehistory. The method can only be used where large pieces of wood survive, generally only in waterlogged environments. The Sweet Track, a neolithic timber walkway in the Somerset Levels, has been dated by this technique to the winter of 3807/3806 BC.

RECONSTRUCTING THE ENVIRONMENT

It is obviously of importance for archaeologists to know something about the environment within which past communities lived. Charred cereals, grain impressions on pottery and the bones of domesticated and wild animals will give some clue to the character of past environments. Cereals, for example, indicate the presence of cleared and cultivated ground, and it is known that pigs and deer favour a woodland habitat. However, more specialised techniques are needed to produce a fuller picture of the vegetational cover of ancient landscapes, and pollen and molluscan (snail) analyses have proved the most successful of these.

Pollen analysis

This technique was first developed in Sweden in 1916 and is now widely used. Pollen is extremely durable and survives very well in acidic and poorly aerated sediments such as lake beds and peat-bogs. Pollen grains belonging to different plant species are very distinctive and easily identifiable under the microscope. By taking samples at intervals throughout a section or core and identifying the presence, absence and differential representation of individual pollen grains at each point, a picture can be built up of the vegetation present at different periods.

Molluscan analysis

Pollen seldom survives on alkaline soils such as those of chalk downland, but the shells of land snails are frequently preserved. Different species of snail favour particular types of environment, whether woodland, open country, boggy ground, cultivated land, and so on. By taking samples for molluscan analysis through the section of a gradually silted ditch, for example, and counting the representation of individual species according to layer, much as is done with pollen analysis, it is possible to reconstruct the changing past environment. Unlike pollen, which can travel great distances on the wind, snail shells will give a picture of very localised environments.

Artefact analysis and experimental archaeology

Artefacts recovered from excavation or fieldwalking can give more than just a date for a site or particular layer. They can tell us about the sort of activities that took place on a site. Large numbers of flint scrapers and knives could indicate the cutting and preparation of hides or skins; a mass of discarded flint flakes might tell of the production of axes or other tools; crucibles and mould fragments of the manufacture of metal implements; animal bones of butchery and feasting; and so on. When such traces are considered in relation to the location of buildings, pits and other features on a settlement a picture of the spatial organisation of tasks can be developed. Furthermore, because people use objects to display their rank and social position it can be possible to say whether a society was egalitarian or stratified, and whether a settlement or burial belonged to a group or individual of a certain social standing. It may also be possible to tell whether an object has been locally manufactured or acquired from a distance by looking at its style or the material from which it is made. This could indicate trade or gift exchange with distant areas. For example, many neolithic stone axes found in south-eastern England have been shown by petrological identification of the rock from which they are made to have come from as far afield as Cornwall and the Lake District.

Valuable clues about life in the past have also come from modern experimentation. At Butser Hill in Hampshire a functioning version of an iron age farm has been set up with the intention of studying the efficiency and problems of ancient farming techniques, cereals and livestock. Replicas of iron age houses have also been built at a number of open-air museums in Britain and illustrate the sophistication of buildings of the period. At West Stow, near Bury St Edmunds in Suffolk, an early Anglo-Saxon settlement was excavated (1965-72) and its timber buildings have been reconstructed on their original sites. Experimentation has been widely used in studies of ancient technology, particularly of flintworking and early metallurgy.

PRESERVATION

Only under exceptional conditions will archaeological remains survive in anything like the state in which they were when deposited. Various **post-depositional processes**, both natural and humanly induced, have an attritional effect on the archaeological record. Preservation is dependent on factors such as the environment in which remains are buried, human disturbance and the resilience of materials to decay.

Small objects of flint and stone, like axes and arrowheads, are virtually indestructible. Most building stone lasts well unless it is soft and exposed to weathering. Once completely covered with soil, stone structures are relatively safe, except for minor disturbances due to tree roots and burrowing animals. One of the finest examples of preservation of stone buildings can be seen at Skara Brae in the Orkneys, where a whole neolithic village constructed entirely of local slate was buried beneath sand dunes until a storm blew the sand away in 1850. Excavated by Professor Gordon Childe in 1928, the village is Orkney's most popular archaeological monument.

Metals vary in their ability to resist decay. Gold is usually found looking as bright and fresh as when it was first buried. Bronze and copper tend to acquire a green patina, which obscures the important fact that when new they looked as bright as gold, whilst iron corrodes badly and in most soils survives only by chance.

Britain's frequently changing climate is not very good for organic preservation. Ideal conditions are to be found in waterlogged soils, lakes, marshes and fens, where an airless (anaerobic) environment prevents bacterial attack (figure 12). At Lake Neuchâtel in Switzerland wooden posts and other organic remains belonging to a number of neolithic lakeside settlements were preserved in the soft waterlogged sediments. Similarly, at Glastonbury and Meare in the Somerset Levels iron age settlements complete with wooden piles and a range of organic domestic utensils survived under the peat. Wooden trackways dating back to the neolithic have also been excavated in that area by Professor John Coles. At Star Carr

12. Bronze age timbers dated to about 1000 BC being excavated at Flag Fen, Peterborough.

in North Yorkshire even older remains survived, in this case a wooden platform of mesolithic date. At the same site bone, antler and horn were also found in fresh condition. These materials will survive in most soils provided that they are not too acidic. In very sandy soils organic materials tend to decay completely, leaving only coloured stains to show where they had once been. In this way wooden posts, coffins and burials require extreme patience in excavation. Bodies at the famous Saxon cemetery of Sutton Hoo (Suffolk) had to be excavated by carefully removing sand from around organic stains where the bones once lay, producing sculpted 'sandmen'.

Oak coffins have survived under some barrows in Yorkshire, but many more are known in an even better state of preservation due to waterlogging in north Germany and Denmark, and their contents can still be seen. The European coffins contained fairly well-preserved bodies, fully clothed, together with ornaments of bronze, leather, wood and bone. In the peat-bogs of the same area objects such as bows and arrows, fishing nets, wooden containers, ploughs and sledges occur; and, most surprisingly, complete and perfect human bodies that may have drowned accidentally or been thrown into the bogs, perhaps as sacrifices or victims of crime. They have all been lightly tanned owing to the presence of tannic acid in the water. The most perfect of these bodies is that known as Grauballe Man. He can be seen in the museum at Moesgaard near Aarhus in Denmark. Parts of three similar corpses, each about two thousand years old, have been found at Lindow Moss in Cheshire: the best-preserved is displayed in the British Museum in London.

Freezing will also permanently preserve organic remains. Burial mounds in the Altai Mountains of Siberia have been frozen since the iron age. They have produced the frozen bodies of a 'princess' and two men covered with black tattooed patterns of fantastic animals, together with skins and carpets with complicated patterns, clothing and footwear. In 1991 the well-preserved body of a late neolithic man who died some 5300 years ago, complete with clothes, a bow and arrow shafts, axe and other equipment, was discovered by chance in melting ice high in the Otztaler Alps on the Austrian-Italian border.

3
Man in Britain

The story of man can be divided into two parts, prehistory and history. The historical part relies on writing to supply the facts. Prehistory belongs to the days before writing and largely relies on the objects produced by early man to piece together his daily life. The further one goes back in time, the scarcer these objects become.

It is probable that Africa was the cradle of mankind, where primitive man emerged as a distinct tool-making species about one and three-quarter million years ago. We do not know when man first reached Britain, but it was not until about half a million years ago that he first began to make tools of stone in southern England and Wales.

LOWER AND MIDDLE PALAEOLITHIC
(Earlier old stone age: 500,000 to 40,000 BC)

During the periods of climatic fluctuation that we call the ice ages, man wandered through western Europe in search of food, moving further north in the warmer periods between the coming of the glaciers, and retreating south again at the approach of the ice sheets. These climatic changes took place over many thousands of years and would not have been perceptible to man living at the time.

As the climate changed, so did the animals available for hunting. In the coldest ice ages there were reindeer, woolly rhinoceroses, mammoths, bison and horses. During the warmest interglacial periods tropical animals such as lions, elephants, monkeys and rhinoceroses roamed Britain. Between times there were the animals which still occupy northern Britain today, like red and fallow deer, highland cattle and rabbits. Rabbits became extinct and were reintroduced by the Normans. Excavations along an ancient river channel at Stanton Harcourt (Oxfordshire) have uncovered the remains of hundreds of mammoths, long-tusked elephants, large bison and numerous other animals, together with the trunks and branches of oak and willow trees.

The great sheets of ice that covered northern Europe caused a worldwide drop in sea level of some 100 metres, thus creating a natural bridge between Britain and Europe for both men and animals throughout much of the old stone age. Since the ice sheets never completely covered Britain it was usually possible for man to wander across the tundra from Hungary, for example, to southern England, in search of animals and birds for food and skins.

Lower and middle palaeolithic man lived in the open air, camping on the shores of lakes and beside rivers, or in the mouths of caves. He lived in small family groups and moved from place to place following the wild animals, and searching for grubs and wild vegetables, much as the Lapps do today. It is unlikely that he had any permanent camp sites, and if he had these would almost certainly have been destroyed by later climatic conditions. All that has survived to the present day are the tools that he made from pieces of stone. These have been found in many places in southern Britain, particularly on the gravel terraces beside rivers. The only known wooden artefact from this period is a spear point, 39 cm long, found on the foreshore at Clacton (Essex).

The stone tools are of two kinds. In one type, rather coarse flakes were struck from a prepared lump of flint and were used for a variety of cutting purposes in a similar fashion to modern knives. The second type of tool is known as a **hand-axe** (for want of a better name). It was made by striking flakes from the flint lump, but retaining the core as the implement. At first these hand-axes were rather crude, but by the time people reached north-west Europe many of them had developed the implements into rather finely chipped pear and oval shapes. They, too, were used for many purposes, including killing animals, cutting meat and leather and grubbing up plant roots and insects. There is nothing to suggest

13. Acheulian hand-axes from the gravels of the Great Ouse: pear-shaped implements on the left, ovates on the right.

that they were ever fixed to wooden handles. It is generally considered that the coarse flake tools belonged to an early simple culture known as **Clactonian**, after the seaside resort where they were first found in the banks of an old channel of the river Thames. The hand-axes, on the other hand, were seen as characteristic of the **Acheulian** culture, which is found all over south-western Europe, in parts of the Near East and southern India and most of Africa (figure 13). It is not clear whether the Clactonian people developed into the Acheulian people, or whether they were replaced by them. However, excavations in recent years, at sites such as Barnham in Suffolk, suggest that both types of tool were contemporary and made by the same manufacturers, the differences being caused by variations in the raw materials and the quality of craftsmanship.

Amongst human skeletal remains from the old stone age in Britain are parts of the back of a skull from Swanscombe in Kent. Fluorine and other tests have confirmed that it is about a quarter of a million years old. The face is missing but it is classified as belonging to *Homo sapiens*, an early form of our own species which is ancestral to modern man (*Homo sapiens sapiens*) and the extinct Neanderthal man, of which the remains of three individuals, an adult and two children, have been found at Pontnewydd Cave in north Wales and dated to 200,000 years ago (plus or minus 25,000 years). In 1994 a human tibia (shin bone) was found during excavations at Boxgrove near Chichester in West Sussex, together with a number of finely made ovate hand-axes. It tells us little about the type of person but it is the oldest human bone yet discovered in Britain (*c.*500,000 years ago).

UPPER PALAEOLITHIC
(*Later old stone age: 40,000 to 8300 BC*)

Broadly speaking, there is a sharp break in Britain between the lower and upper palaeolithic cultures. People of the upper palaeolithic have left hundreds of specialist tools fashioned from fine parallel-sided flint blades. These were used for scraping and boring holes, as gouges and knives. At the same time tools were made from bone, antler and ivory, whilst a great many must have been made from wood, although these have seldom survived.

The people who made these tools all belonged to the race of modern man known as ***Homo sapiens sapiens***. They lived in small family groups in the mouths of caves or in lightly constructed shelters of branches and skins. They were familiar with fire for heat, light and cooking and used fur and leather for clothes. Heat and clothing made it easier for them to survive the long icy winters. They ornamented themselves with necklaces and bangles made from perforated animal teeth, small carved bones and shells. A

14. The Victoria Cave above Settle in North Yorkshire was occupied by animals and man during the upper palaeolithic period.

curious object of deer antler with a hole bored through its widest end, and known to us as a *baton de commandement*, may have been some kind of status symbol.

Two cultural groups of upper palaeolithic people can be clearly recognised in Britain. They seem to have been separated in time by a period of between ten thousand and fifteen thousand years, during which the last ice age reached its most severe conditions. Traces of the earlier of these groups, preceding the last glaciation, have been found in Wales in the Ffynnon Beuno and Cae Gwyn caves on the eastern side of the Vale of Clwyd, at Goat's Cave, Paviland, in the Gower peninsula, and at Kent's Cavern, Torquay (Devon). At Goat's Cave bones of mammoth, cave bear, woolly rhinoceros, elk and hyena were found, and the ceremonial burial of a young man whose corpse had been smeared with red ochre, perhaps in an attempt to bring the appearance of life back to the body.

The other cultural group, following the coldest part of the last ice age, the **Creswellian**, is named after Creswell Crags in Derbyshire and flourished in a number of cave sites in Britain, including Gough's Cave and Flint Jack's Cave at Cheddar, the Hyena Den at Wookey and Aveline's Hole (all in Somerset); at Kent's Cavern, Torquay (Devon); the Victoria Cave, Settle (North Yorkshire) (figure 14); and Church Hole, Mother Grundy's Parlour, Pin Hole, and Robin Hood's Cave at Creswell. The last three caves contained the only specimens of palaeolithic art yet found in Britain; these are all engravings on bone and include a horse's head, reindeer and a stylised human figure.

MESOLITHIC BRITAIN
(Middle stone age: 8300 to 4000 BC)

With the final withdrawal of the ice sheets in Britain, the climate became steadily warmer and over a period of thousands of years the sparse tundra gave way to steppe-like vegetation with alder and hazel scrub. This in turn was replaced by birch and pine woods and then heavy oak, elm, hazel and lime forests. Towards the end of this time, about 6500 BC, Britain once more became an island, separated from the European mainland by a wide English Channel.

Some of the Creswellians of the upper palaeolithic continued to live in their upland caves in Derbyshire, and at Uxbridge in Middlesex and Staines in Surrey late upper palaeolithic hunting sites also remained in use into the mesolithic era. For the most part north European people moved westwards into Britain from Denmark and the Baltic. They belonged to the **Maglemosian** culture, which was well adapted for life in forests and along the marshy edges of lakes and streams, which were then more extensive than today. There they could hunt, fowl and fish. Their equipment consisted of antler spearheads, arrows with minute flint tips (called **microliths**) (figure 15) and barbed harpoon heads of bone and antler for

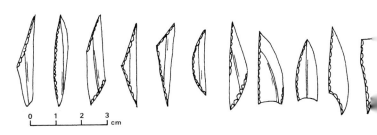

0   1   2   3 cm

15. A selection of flint microliths.

spearing fish. They used a variety of scrapers for cleaning and cutting meat and skins and for woodworking, and parallel-sided heavy flint axes and adzes for felling and shaping tree-trunks. A few of their huts have been found at Abinger and Farnham in Surrey, Broom Hill and Bowman's Farm in Hampshire, and at Deepcar in South Yorkshire. They consisted of oval scoops in the gravel screened with branches and skins.

Since none are known from Britain, we have to look to Scandinavia for information about complex burial rituals. Excavations at Vedbaek, 20 km north of Copenhagen in Denmark, have revealed a mesolithic cemetery laid out in parallel rows, containing twenty-two burials, seventeen adults and five children. The men had been equipped with bone daggers and flint blades, the women with jewellery of perforated deer and boar teeth. A new-born baby had been laid on a swan's wing. The heads and clothes of most of the bodies had been smeared with red ochre, which had stained the soil in the graves. At the Skateholm cemetery in southern Sweden a number of burials were accompanied by their hunting dogs, some of which had been deliberately killed. Other dogs had been individually buried with rich grave goods, including flint blades and antlers, suggesting that they were highly regarded by their owners.

At **Star Carr** in North Yorkshire excavations revealed a rough platform of branches beside a lake, on which mesolithic hunters had lived during the late spring and early summer. Owing to the waterlogged nature of the site stag-antler spearheads and elk-antler mattocks had survived together with beads of perforated amber, lias and deer teeth; wood had also been preserved, and rolls of birch bark from which various containers were made, together with large quantities of bracket fungus for tinder. Twenty-one stag frontlets, with parts of their antlers remaining, had been perforated through the forehead and may have been worn as masks for deer stalking, or in some magical hunting dance, like that surviving in the horn dance of Abbots Bromley in Staffordshire. Star Carr was almost certainly a temporary hunting camp rather than a permanently occupied base settlement.

The extensive forest cover brought new animals into Britain. Wild pig, red and roe deer, elk and ox provided food; but the huntsman also had to watch out for the wolf, brown bear, wild cat and otter, some of which could provide valuable skins for clothing. The dog was already domesticated in Britain by this time.

Canoes hollowed out from tree-trunks, and perhaps of birch bark like those of the North American Indians, were used for fishing and were paddled across lakes and rivers, the waterways providing man's main routes for travel.

Around 6500 BC new types of flint microliths appeared in Britain and western Europe. The blades were smaller and occurred in a greater variety of shapes, probably indicating new types of arrows. Sometimes the microliths were glued with resin into wooden hafts, whilst others were glued in rows along a handle to form a saw-like edge, or used as tips for drills. Archaeologists have not yet given a name to these late mesolithic changes. Like all mesolithic folk, the people who were responsible for the new flints relied on hunting, fishing and gathering wild fruits for their livelihood and moved about from place to place, leaving no permanent mark on the countryside.

Along the west coast of Scotland a series of shell middens, the refuse from simple domestic settlements, suggest a more settled way of life. Objects of antler and bone indicate that their makers had adapted themselves to a specialised economy based on coastal fishing and hunting. Limpets seem to have been eaten in large numbers, together with crab, oyster, lobster and periwinkle. Long parallel-sided stone tools have been recognised as limpet scoops for prising the limpets from rocks. These western Scottish groups are known as **Obanians** after the first sites found near Oban in Argyll. Any coastal settlements in southern Britain during the later mesolithic have probably been destroyed by changes in sea level.

THE NEOLITHIC PERIOD
(New stone age: 4000 to 2200 BC)

There are a number of features that distinguish the neolithic period from those that went before. They include the production of polished stone tools, the manufacture of pottery, the domestication of animals and plants, and the construction of communal monuments. During the later sixth millennium BC these innovations were spread by pioneering groups over much of central and western Europe from the north-eastern Mediterranean. By about 5000 BC they had reached the Channel coast and in due course spread along the whole of the European seaboard from Jutland to the mouth of the Loire.

In the forests of Britain the indigenous mesolithic hunter-gatherers remained largely undisturbed by these continental movements until about 4000 BC and then, fairly suddenly, signs of neolithic culture rapidly appeared throughout the British Isles. Whether this was the result of colonisation from across the Channel, as has long been believed, or the expedient adoption by the aborigines of new continental ideas resulting from cross-channel contact is open to debate. It is certain, however, that none of these new ideas could have been practised in Britain without extensive training in the complexities of animal husbandry, crop cultivation, the construction and firing of pottery, and the initial provision from Europe of seed corn, stock animals and specimen pots.

These first agriculturalists are found in many parts of the British Isles after 4000 BC and soon spread along river valleys and over chalk downlands. Here, those who chose could clear the lightly wooded gravels and chalk hillslopes to cultivate wheat and barley and graze their herds, whilst others could continue to practise their traditional hunting skills along the coasts and uplands. Some prospected in highland Britain for suitable stone for polished axe production. There was room for all. Soon it became clear that the ability to control the growth of food at will meant that at last, if they chose, people could be freed from a wandering life dependent on hunting and fishing. They could choose to live in one locality, where they could build durable houses, and it was easier and safer to produce larger families. In time they would clear more forest and bring more land under cultivation.

Waterlogged sites in western Europe tell us that the earliest farmers were skilled woodworkers, though few traces of their prowess survive in Britain. Isolated permanent houses belonging to the earliest farmers have been discovered at Fengate near Peterborough, Hembury and Haldon in Devon and at Lismore Fields near Buxton in Derbyshire. Numerous groups of pits containing neolithic refuse have been found at Hurst Fen in Suffolk and elsewhere. The houses were usually small and rectangular with timber walls and thatched roofs. They were often of a temporary nature. Their footings were so shallow that they could easily have been destroyed by ploughing, which may explain why so few have been found. Scatters of flints and perhaps sherds of pottery lying on a field surface may give the best clue to the site of a house. It seems probable that they ranged across the countryside in isolated croft-like clusters. It is likely that the farmers left their homesteads from time to time and wandered with their herds to the best pastures, returning home at planting and harvest times. Their primitive hoe agriculture, which included chopping down

16. The three concentric rings of ditches at the Windmill Hill causewayed enclosure in Wiltshire, seen from the air.

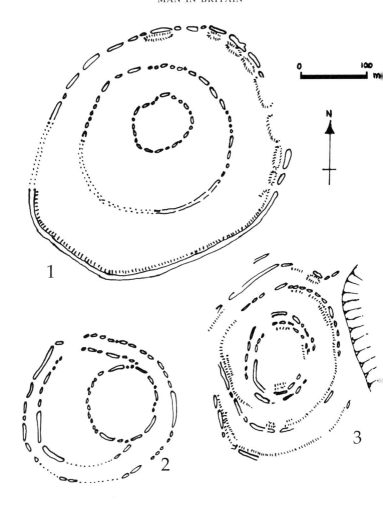

17. *Plans of causewayed enclosures: 1 Windmill Hill (Wiltshire); 2 Briar Hill (Northamptonshire); 3 Whitehawk Camp (Sussex).*

and burning scrub and planting seeds in the ashes, would eventually exhaust the land and force them to seek new ground. It is likely that the majority moved only within a restricted local area, always returning to their ancestral communal monuments.

Of these, large enclosures, often on hilltops and surrounded by woodland, were formed by digging one or more concentric rings of quarry ditches. The material obtained was piled up to make internal banks (often revetted with wood). The ditches were broken by frequent causeways or gaps of undug subsoil and are called **causewayed enclosures** (figure 16). Although similar sites are known along the western seaboard of Europe from southern Sweden to the Charente, they are probably best-known in England, where more than sixty have been identified. They seem to have been constructed between 3700 and 3200 BC (figure 17).

Their function seems to have been extremely complex and is still poorly understood. Extensive groups of pits and postholes in some of the enclosures, such as Hambledon Hill (Dorset), Hembury (Devon) and Crickley Hill (Gloucestershire), suggest that those may have contained settlements of some kind. In the majority of cases, however, there is little evidence to indicate that they were permanently occupied. Instead, amongst the rubbish thrown into the ditches have been found numerous axes of non-local stone and pottery tempered with grit not occurring in the vicinity of the camp, suggesting that these items were brought by people from a considerable distance, who congregated seasonally within the enclosure for some social, religious or economic purpose which may have resembled the fairs of medieval England.

There is firm evidence to show that sometimes these sites also served defensive and mortuary functions. The size of many of the enclosures makes it clear that they were built and used by large numbers of people, family and lineage groups perhaps being responsible for digging separate ditch sections. The broken pottery found in the ditches belonged to round-bottomed baggy-shaped vessels of the Plain Bowl Culture, which can be divided into at least four regional groupings and first appears in Britain about 3600 BC (figure 18). With it have been found polished flint axes, leaf-shaped arrowheads, scrapers for cleaning skins and various flint points for wood and leather working. The pottery and tools could have been used for practical and ritual purposes before being discarded in the ditches, perhaps as part of some depositional ceremony. The burials of complete cattle, showing no signs of dismemberment, and scatters of carefully cleaned and buried animal bones stretching for many meters along the ditch bottom suggest a similar purpose. Human skulls without mandibles have been found deliberately positioned in the ditches at Etton (Cam-

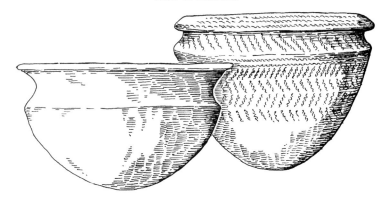

18. Round-bottomed plain bowl of Grimston type and a decorated Peterborough pot, both about 23 cm in diameter.

bridgeshire) and Hambledon Hill (Dorset), perhaps so placed to ward off evil spirits. In the interior of the latter site numerous human bodies had been exposed to the elements, slowly decaying and disintegrating. One can imagine the noise and stench as scavenging birds and animals pecked over the cadavers at this windswept hilltop excarnation site.

At Crickley Hill the enclosure was heavily attacked with bows and arrows, the remains of the latter having been found embedded in the entrance. Similarly at Hembury archers used leaf-shaped arrowheads in their assault before deliberately destroying the structure with fire.

Communal effort is also demonstrated by the construction of **earthen** (or **non-megalithic**) **long barrows**, of which about 260 are known, mostly in central southern and north-east England. These were usually rectangular or trapezoidal mounds of earth up to 3 metres high and between 15 and 125 metres long (average 50 metres), usually higher at the broader eastern end, and frequently with quarry ditches along each side. Long before the mound building began, a rectangular mortuary enclosure or a box-like chamber of wood or turf, possibly with a removable lid or roof, was set in place, as at Fussell's Lodge (Wiltshire) or Haddenham (Cambridgeshire). Into these over many years might be placed between one and fifty burials. Often, though not invariably, the flesh had clearly rotted away before the jumbled bones, often lacking skulls, and without specific grave goods, were placed in the chamber. This again suggests excarnation, perhaps in a nearby causewayed enclosure. More burials would have been added to the chamber until the time came finally to seal it beneath a covering mound, after which the timber would begin to rot and eventually collapse. The long barrow often had an elaborate timber façade at the higher end, where scattered animal bones and broken pots suggest that funeral feasts and ceremonies took place from time to time. Sometimes the decaying corpses were partially cremated before burial, and occasionally, as at Nutbane (Hampshire), the whole mortuary chamber was ignited before being covered by the barrow mound.

It has been possible to show that the later long barrows, such as examples at Maxey (Cambridgeshire), Barrow Hills (Oxfordshire) and Easton Down (Wiltshire), contained very few burials, or just a single one, usually male. It is quite clear that only a small fraction of the neolithic population was buried under long barrows, and then they might be represented by only a few selected bones. What criteria existed for an individual's inclusion in a tomb we shall never know. They may have been representatives of a local hierarchy: they certainly included children. It was quite common for some neolithic burials on river gravels and on the Yorkshire Wolds, early in the third millennium, to be covered by round barrows and the custom was to spread to the southern chalk downs during the next two hundred years.

The earthen long barrows are found mainly on the chalk hills, especially in Wessex, Sussex, Lincolnshire and East Yorkshire, often situated close to prehistoric trackways, some of which, like the Ridgeway and Icknield Way, are still in use today. In fenland areas wooden trackways were laid for considerable distances across marshy ground. The Sweet Track, one of a number uncovered during peat digging in the Somerset Levels, has been dated by dendrochronology to 3806 BC.

Long barrows were also constructed in the stone-producing areas of western Britain. In those parts the wooden mortuary chambers under the earthen long barrows were copied using large blocks of stone (**megaliths**). Traditionally called **gallery graves** (figure 19), although no longer seen as a united group, these tombs consist of a long stone passage which is either divided into sections with cross-slabs or has small chambers on either side. It is covered by a long wedge-shaped (or occasionally circular) mound of earth or stones, which is considerably longer than the tomb passage within. The passage entrance opens at the wider end of the mound on to a curved forecourt. It was here that funeral feasts took place and offerings for the dead were deposited. A large slab of stone normally sealed the entrance to the tomb. Unlike the wooden chambers in the earthen long barrows, which

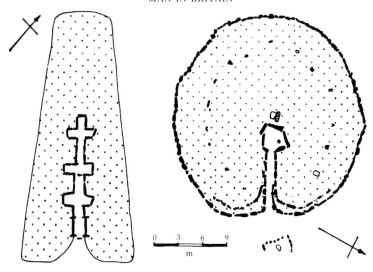

*19. (Left) Plan of a gallery grave at Stoney Littleton (Somerset).
(Right) A passage grave: Bryn Celli Ddu in Anglesey.*

would have begun to rot after about ten years, the stone gallery
graves could remain accessible and in use for hundreds of years.
During that time many new corpses and funerary deposits would
be added, whilst older material might be moved to the back of the
tomb or discarded.

A group of gallery graves defined as the **Cotswold-Severn
tombs** is found on either side of the Severn estuary, in south
Wales, the Mendips, the Cotswolds and north Wiltshire and
Oxfordshire. Of these the most accessible is undoubtedly that at
West Kennet near Avebury in Wiltshire (figure 20). One of the
largest chambered barrows in Britain, its mound is 100 metres
long and 2.4 metres high, although the burial chamber at its
eastern end is only 12 metres long. Two transverse chambers lie
on either side of the central passage, which ends in a rectangular
chamber. Three large stones, one of them 3.6 metres high, blocked
the entrance after the last burials had taken place. Excavations
1955-6 showed that skeletal remains of about thirty adults and
children remained in the tomb, together with pots similar to those
found at the Windmill Hill causewayed enclosure 3 km to the
north. Other gallery graves well worth visiting include Hetty

20. *Interior of the West Kennet long barrow in Wiltshire during reconstruction. Two burial chambers lie on either side of the passage, and one at the end.*

Peggler's Tump, Uley, and Nympsfield (figure 21), both in Gloucestershire, Wayland's Smithy in south Oxfordshire and Stoney Littleton in Somerset (figure 19).

Some Cotswold tombs have lateral or side chambers which

21. *The gallery grave at Nympsfield (Gloucestershire) showing the curved forecourt. The capstones have been missing for centuries.*

were entered from the long sides of the barrow and sealed when full. Hazleton North in Gloucestershire is an example that was totally excavated in 1979-82 prior to destruction. The trapezoidal cairn was 53 metres long and 19 metres wide at the broader west end. It was built of limestone from two irregular quarry pits close by. Near its centre, and entered from opposite long sides, were two L-shaped chambers. The southern one had human bones scattered throughout its length. Mostly disarticulated, they represented fourteen adults and between six and eleven children, of both sexes. In the north chamber were the remains of twenty-one adults and twelve to nineteen children. The final adult male burial lay just inside the entrance with flint-knapping equipment in his hands. Earlier burials had been moved to the sides to make subsequent access easier, and there were indications that skulls and long bones had been partially sorted. Alan Saville, the excavator, has suggested that the Cotswold-Severn tombs may have served local communities for quite short periods, perhaps less than a hundred years, and that they may all have been built between *c*.3800 and 3500 BC. One of the Hazleton burial chambers has been reconstructed in Cirencester Museum.

Belas Knap near Winchcombe in Gloucestershire is a beautifully rebuilt example of a similar tomb with a false doorway or **portal** at its higher, wider end, and four burial chambers that were originally completely enclosed but are now accessible from the sides. They contained at least thirty-eight skeletons.

Related groups of gallery graves exist in north-west Wales, the Peak District, Cornwall and the Isle of Man and may have given rise to similar tombs in Ireland and south-west Scotland.

There are some forty long parallel-sided banked and ditched enclosures, apparently without entrances, called **cursuses**. These seem to be connected with funeral ritual and are often laid out so that they deliberately incorporate a long barrow. One near Stonehenge is 2.8 km long, and the external parallel ditches are 100 metres apart. An even bigger one in Dorset is 9.7 km long with external ditches 82 metres apart. Cursuses may have been some kind of processional way allowing the spirits of the dead exclusive passage through a ceremonial landscape. They may have been the forerunners of the stone rows of later neolithic times. One at Drayton (Oxfordshire) dates between 3635 and 3385 BC, though most seem to be nearer 3000 BC.

Also related to the cursuses are the **bank barrows** of Dorset. These were very extensive long barrows. One at Maiden Castle was 546 metres long and at its eastern end covered the burials of two neolithic children, both six or seven years old, together with a small pottery cup. Perhaps they were dedicatory or sacrificial deposits. A dismembered body found in the bank barrow, and once thought to be neolithic, has been shown to be of Saxon date. Other bank barrows can be observed on Martin's Down, Long Bredy, and in Broadmayne parish, all in Dorset.

It is important to remember that when the barrows and other neolithic monuments had completed their active life they did not disappear. They remained monuments in the landscape. Many were revered: they were associated with the spirits of the ancestors and as such were often incorporated into later projects.

Most of the basic equipment of the neolithic period was made from clay, wood or flint. A few wooden objects have survived such as axe handles, a plough ard, a bow and a carved human figure from the Somerset Levels. In contrast there are vast assemblages of flint work in museums, showing that, whilst pottery varied from one part of Britain to another, the flint tool kit remained basically the same everywhere: polished axes, leaf-shaped arrowheads, convex scrapers, sickle blades, knives and a few other types.

The best flint was obtained by digging **flint mines**. Surface flint was usually inferior for making fine-quality implements, having been damaged by annual frost action. Shafts were sunk through the upper chalk, often to depths of 10 or 14 metres, in order to reach better-quality flint nodules that lay below ground. At the bottom of the shafts galleries fanned out to exploit the flint seams to the full. It has been estimated that it would have taken six months to dig a shaft, and about a fortnight for each gallery. Because of the limited size of the mine, no more than ten people could have worked there. One or two men would have worked at the flint face, others would have loaded the raw material into baskets whilst more would have hauled it to the surface. Work in the galleries would have been limited by lack of fresh air and poor lighting, whilst the flint and chalk dust would have taken its toll of miners by causing early death from bronchial complaints, just as it did in more recently worked flint mines. Some mines could have produced as much as 40 tonnes of flint. Once one shaft had been exhausted, another was dug nearby, the waste material from it being tipped into the disused shaft (figure 22).

Tools used in the mining included wooden or scapula shovels and red-deer antlers. Two mineshafts at Grimes Graves in Norfolk produced 244 antlers. The bulk of these antlers were cast from deer and not cut from hunted animals. This suggests that the miners herded the animals in the forests around the mines. The antlers were driven into the chalk with flint hammerstones and then used as levers to force the blocks out. Further antlers were used to rake the waste chalk and flint lumps into baskets, which

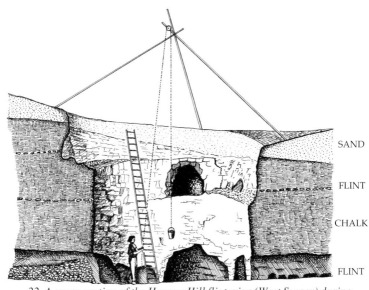

22. A cross-section of the Harrow Hill flint mine (West Sussex) during excavation. Upper and lower galleries have been dug to obtain flint at both levels. (After R. Gurd.)

were hauled to the surface on ropes and dumped at the pithead. The nodules of flint were carried to working places not far from the mouths of the mineshafts. There they were worked into the required shapes and then distributed by hand to hand exchange all over Britain, many of them eventually finding their way to the causewayed enclosure celebrations. It has recently been suggested that flint mines were dug purely for ritual purposes. Economically, this seems most unlikely.

Flint mines have been found and some excavated in a number of chalk areas of southern England. The oldest were in Sussex at Church Hill, Findon, and Blackpatch, dating from around 3800 to 3500 BC. Others at Cissbury, Harrow Hill and Stoke Down in Sussex and Easton Down in Wiltshire are later. The largest and best-known group of more than six hundred open-cast and deep-shaft workings occupies 13.5 hectares at **Grimes Graves** in Norfolk, 5 km north-east of Brandon. It was being worked on a seasonal basis, probably determined by the agricultural calendar, during the later neolithic period and earlier bronze age, between 3000 and 1900 BC. One badly damaged shaft, excavated in 1914, is accessible to visitors. Another mine, no longer open to the public, seems to have contained flint of poorer quality and, on abandoning it, the miners left at the bottom offerings of good-quality flint blocks arranged in a triangle, seven antler picks, some of which appear to have been deliberately broken, pieces of grooved ware pottery and a chalk lamp. Perhaps these were deposited as a hint to some spiritual earth god to make the next shaft more productive!

In western Britain during the fourth millennium BC neolithic folk began to quarry natural rock outcrops in order to produce **polished stone axes** (figure 23). They recognised a need for efficient tools that would speed up forest clearance for agriculture and enable wooden rollers, levers and scaffolding to be quickly produced for stone tomb building and carpentry in general. Although it is clear that the bulk of stone axes were used in that way, it is also known that some had a special symbolic significance. They were often beautifully made, sometimes of exotic materials like jadeite, and must have served a ceremonial purpose before being deposited in specially selected places from which they were not expected to be recovered. Wherever suitable rocks outcropped, axes were roughed out and polished and then distributed across Britain, either by direct trade, possibly in bulk (and by boat), or by exchange from one person to another, in many short exchanges like a prolonged game of passing the parcel. The polished axes were tough and obviously competed with the flint axes, for they occur all over the 'flint' areas of southern England. Axes quarried around 3700 BC at Great Langdale in Cumbria travelled to central and eastern England; from Cornwall they reached Wessex and East Anglia; from Craig Lwyd in Gwynedd (figure 24) they have been

23. Neolithic polished stone axes.

PENMAENMAWR

24. Stone axes quarried around Penmaenmawr (Craig Lwyd) in north Wales were widely distributed across England and Wales. (After Clough and Cummins, 1988.)

25. The entrance to the passage grave of Bryn Celli Ddu in Anglesey. Notice the kerb of stones retaining the mound.

found in Wales and as far as the Windmill Hill causewayed enclosure in Wiltshire, showing that they were being distributed between 3400 and 3200 BC. Axes from Rathlin Island and Tievebulliagh in County Antrim are concentrated in Ulster, but some crossed the Irish Sea and travelled as far south as the London region.

THE PASSAGE-GRAVE BUILDERS

Some time before 4000 BC a new type of great stone tomb, known as a passage grave, appeared in southern Brittany. Soon afterwards examples were appearing in Spain and Portugal and in western Ireland. By 3000 BC the idea had spread to north Wales.

Passage graves are circular mounds of earth or stone containing one or two round or polygonal burial chambers with corbelled roofs, entered from outside by long narrow passages (figure 25). They are usually built on hilltops in commanding positions and are often grouped in cemeteries. The finest groups are in Ireland, where more than three hundred still exist. They vary in size from the small and early cairns on Carrowmore and Carrowkeel Mountain in County Sligo, about 3 metres high and 12 metres in diameter, to the great tombs of the Boyne valley in County Meath, at Knowth, Dowth and New Grange. The last, now reconstructed, still stands 12 metres high and between 80 and 85 metres in diameter, with the remains of a circle that once contained thirty-eight great stones standing around it. Radiocarbon dates suggest that it was built about 3200 BC. A curious slot in the roof of the entrance passage allows the

49

26. Looking along the passage of Bryn Celli Ddu into the burial chamber. There is a low bench on the right-hand side of the passage.

sun for a few minutes at dawn on midwinter's morning to enter the burial chamber and warm the ashes of the dead: surely a link with sun worship. The same phenomenon occurs at the Maes Howe passage grave in the Orkney Islands.

A small fringe group of passage graves mirrors the Boyne tombs in north Wales. The two finest examples are on Anglesey. Of these Bryn Celli Ddu is a mound 27 metres in diameter and 3.6 metres high covering a short passage 8 metres long, at the end of which is a polygonal chamber some 2.4 metres across. Standing in it is a single upright stone which may be of phallic significance. Skeletons and cremated bones were found in the chamber (figures 19 and 26). Also on Anglesey is Barclodiad y Gawres. This passage grave is covered by a modern concrete dome which protects the original 6 metres long stone passage, at the end of which is a cross-shaped chamber. Five of the wallstones of the chamber are decorated with stylised carvings: lozenges, spirals and zigzags (figure 27). Similar

27. (Opposite page) A decorated stone from Barclodiad y Gawres passage grave in Anglesey. The decoration may have been made with a flint punch and wooden mallet.

28. *Mulfra Quoit, south of Zennor in Cornwall, is a portal dolmen whose capstone has slipped backwards. It was once covered with a mound of earth and stones.*

29. *The remains of the Medway burial chamber known as Kit's Coty House near Aylesford in Kent.*

decoration occurs in a number of the Irish and French passage graves, and two stones at Bryn Celli Ddu also have carving on them. Passage and gallery graves are amongst the most evocative archaeological sites to visit.

Other regional groups of stone burial chambers existed. In Wales and Cornwall tombs looking like high tables with vertical wall-stones and a sloping top are known as **portal dolmens** (figure 28). Almost certainly once covered by a cairn of stones, they are typified by Pentre Ifan in Pembrokeshire and Trethevy Quoit in Cornwall. A small group of burial chambers set at the extreme end of long, narrow, rectangular barrows close to the Medway in Kent shows similarities to north German and Scandinavian tombs. The most famous site in the group is Kit's Coty House near Aylesford. The covering mound of this barrow has long since been destroyed but three large upright wallstones and a capstone survive, in spite of modern vandalism (figure 29). More complete Medway sites can be seen at Coldrum, not far from Trottiscliffe, and at The Chestnuts, Addington, both in Kent.

It was during the later neolithic, between 3000 and 2000 BC, that a form of **rock art** developed in northern Britain and many parts of Ireland. It most commonly takes the form of **cup and ring** marks. These are small circular cup-like depressions surrounded by one or more hollowed rings, pecked into the surface of standing stones, the interiors of burial cists, and most commonly on outcrops of living rock from Derbyshire north to Orkney. Spirals, rectangles, lozenges and grid patterns often occur alongside the cup marks, linked together to form much more complex, but apparently abstract, designs. The simpler patterns tend to be found on isolated boulders, scattered over now barren moorlands, where they may once have acted as direction indicators. The climate would have made these moorlands much more habitable in neolithic times. The complex designs tend to cover several square metres and occur on larger horizontal or gently sloping rock outcrops, although vertical surfaces are by no means unknown. These outcrops tend to be peripheral to areas of occupation, and in some places are intervisible with each other. There is no evidence that the designs covering a rock surface are all contemporary. Indeed, patterns may have been added and developed over many years, changing with current fashion, like graffiti at a bus stop!

Sometimes decorated stones have been found inside early bronze age burial cairns. In most cases these seem to be reused, suggesting that the stone had some special religious, magical or hereditary tenurial significance important to the well-being of the deceased. The reuse of decorated stones is well-known in some of the megalithic tombs of Brittany.

Innumerable attempts to explain British rock art simply as doodles, graffiti, maps, games or coded messages are purely subjective. Whilst a religious symbolism, loosely connected with the fertility of the land and sea and its occupants, seems logical, the final solution probably lies in a combination of elements from most of the above, and a few not yet considered.

By the second half of the third millennium BC a number of changes in neolithic life can be detected, perhaps resulting from some kind of crisis or tension between different groups. By that time the ditches of most causewayed enclosures had finally silted up, though the sites had not been totally abandoned and were still being utilised from time to time as their function lingered in folk memory. Burial in round barrows began to proliferate, particularly in northern Britain. Passage graves made a final appearance in the Isles of Scilly, where about fifty diminutive chambered tombs (with four on the Cornish mainland) are known as **entrance graves** (figure 30). In these the chamber opens straight out of the side of the circular mound. All the entrance graves are small, seldom more than 7.5 metres in diameter and 3 metres high (though one exception on the island of Gugh is 23 metres in diameter).

The earliest pottery vessels made in Britain, plain open bowls with slight carinations (shoulders) and round bases, appeared by

30. The Chapel Euny entrance grave at Brane in Cornwall.

3600 BC. From these, regional styles developed with simple decoration, including Windmill Hill, Mildenhall and Abingdon wares. By 3000 BC **Peterborough wares** dominated. These tended to consist of rather coarse round-bottomed bowls, almost entirely covered with impressed decoration, and included regional variations such as Mortlake and Fengate wares. Later in the third millennium BC **grooved ware** pottery was produced. This probably originated in northern Britain but became widespread in the south. It is often associated with henge monuments. The pots had flat bases and almost vertical sides richly decorated with panels of incised straight lines and chevrons. The stone and bone tools of the earlier neolithic remained in use, with hunting and fishing continuing to play some part in the life of the later neolithic people. The only major change was the substitution of transverse arrowheads for the leaf-shaped variety. Instead of being pointed, the tip of the new head was formed by a broad sharp blade.

The economy of the later neolithic was based on garden-scale agriculture and domestic livestock, with an increase in pig production. As in the earlier neolithic, evidence for settlements is lacking, though pits and 'floors' are often recorded. At Mount Pleasant (Glamorgan) and Ronaldsway in the Isle of Man single rectangular homesteads have been found. Two small square huts at Trelyston (Powys) have produced flints and grooved ware. In Orkney a number of nucleated stone-built settlements, also using grooved ware pottery, have been excavated. They include Skara Brae, Barnhouse, Rinyo and Links of Notland. Such limited evidence may well suggest that we are in part still dealing with itinerant communities. However, at Fengate near Peterborough rectangular fields, separated by ditched droveways, and a house suggest that some permanent and well-organised farms were in existence.

Throughout the third millennium BC a new type of field monument, known as a **henge**, developed in late neolithic Britain, first appearing on the lowland river gravels. It has been suggested that it probably replaced the earlier causewayed enclosures, and the radiocarbon dates obtained from some of the excavated sites tend to support this. Henges were circular banked enclosures with internal ditches, and sometimes inner settings of pits, posts or stones. The bank and ditch are usually broken by a single entrance, although double- and four-entrance henges do exist. The ditch often seems to have been dug as a series of pits later joined together, a similar method to that employed in the causewayed enclosures. One of the earliest single-entrance henges in Britain is at Arminghall near Norwich. It contained a horseshoe-shaped setting of eight massive oak posts and can be dated to 2490 BC. Woodhenge, near Amesbury in Wiltshire, contained six concentric rings of wooden posts within

31. A general view of Stonehenge from the north.

a ditched enclosure 74 metres in diameter. Stuart Piggott suggested that these formed the uprights of a circular wooden building. In the centre was the skeleton of a three-year-old child with its skull cleft by an axe, perhaps a dedicatory or sacrificial burial. Similar circular structures have been excavated in enormous henge monuments at Durrington Walls (Wiltshire) and Mount Pleasant (Dorset). They may have been tribal meeting places like those used by the Creek and Cherokee Indians of the south-eastern United States in the eighteenth century AD.

Amongst other single-entrance henges are the Stripple Stones on Bodmin Moor (Cornwall), which has a setting of fifteen stones, and Gorsey Bigbury in Somerset, with no visible internal features.

Stonehenge gave part of its name to henge monuments, although it predates them by several hundred years (figure 31). It is a unique monument in many ways, which developed steadily over 1500 years. A recent reappraisal has divided this development into three main phases (figure 32).

In Phase 1 (*c.*2950-2900 BC) a circular ditch, 107 metres in diameter, was dug, made up of about sixty irregular linked segments. The excavated chalk was thrown up to form a substantial internal bank, and a slight external one. Two clear entrance gaps were left, one 11 metres wide at the north-east, and another 3 metres wide on the south side. Inside the earthwork a ring of fifty-six pits, now called the Aubrey Holes, was dug. It is quite feasible, though by no means certain, that they initially held stout wooden posts, which would have formed a notable feature in the landscape. If this was the case, they were removed before they had time to decay in their holes.

During Phase 2 (*c.*2900-2600 BC) the circular ditch silted up, and parts of it were deliberately backfilled. In the centre of the monument a large timber feature was set up. Unfortunately later

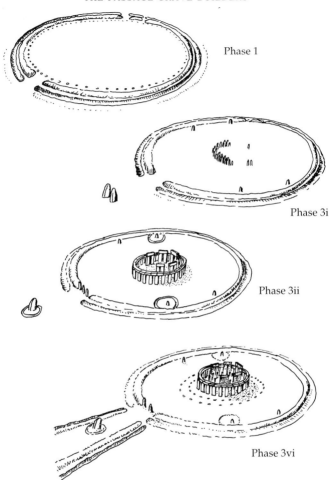

32. *Four phases in the development of Stonehenge: Phase 1 about 2900 BC; Phase 3i about 2600 BC; Phase 3ii about 2300 BC; and Phase 3vi around 2000 BC.*

disturbance has destroyed most of the evidence for this, and we can no longer make any sense of it. A double line of posts led from the centre towards the southern entrance. Near the end of Phase 2

33. The great trilithons (three stones) at Stonehenge. The careful shaping of the stones is clearly visible.

small deposits of cremated human bones, perhaps held in leather bags, were inserted into the top of most of the Aubrey Holes.

Phase 3i began about 2600 BC with the arrival of more than 120 blocks of bluestone from the Prescelly Mountains of Pembrokeshire and their erection in a double circle, which may never have been completed. In less than three hundred years it was dismantled. Whether the bluestones reached Wessex by the process of glaciation or alternatively were quarried in Wales and brought by man is a subject of continuing debate. If the latter is true, then the prominent dolerite mountains of Prescelly, heralding the last land stage of the trade route from Wessex to the copper and tin deposits in Ireland, may have been regarded with a certain religious awe: perhaps they were considered to be sacred mountains. At any rate some strong central authority must have existed to plan such a complicated engineering operation, which involved dragging the 123 stones from Prescelly to the sea, floating them on rafts to the mouth of the Bristol Avon, then up that river and its tributary the Frome; from there overland to the Wylye, by raft again down the Wylye and up the Wiltshire Avon to Amesbury and overland to Stonehenge. Experiments have been carried out which show that this journey was possible. If true, it would have happened about 2600 BC. Outside the north-east entrance two rough blocks of sarsen stone, one called the Heelstone, were set in place.

In Phase 3ii, about 2300 BC many great blocks of sarsen stone were dragged from the Marlborough Downs, some 32 km to the north, where they occur naturally on the hillside. They were shaped and erected in a lintelled circle which enclosed five trilithons (literally three stones, two uprights and one across the top) (figure 33). Architectural refinements included groove-and-tongue and mortice-and-tenon joints for attaching lintel stones to one another and to their uprights – all carpentry techniques familiar to people

58

used to working in wood. All the upright stones were carefully smoothed and had an entasis, that is a deliberate swelling halfway up the stone. This was a device later used in classical architecture to counteract the effects of perspective. This is a remarkable refinement to find at this time in a European offshore island. A carving on one of the trilithons (stone number 53) represents a hilted dagger, and a number of the other stones have carvings of metal axeheads upon them. Were these early masons' marks, or the sign of an axe cult? Axes have certainly been found carved on cairn stones in Argyll and Dorset, and the practice may have its origins in Brittany, where axe carvings are well represented in chambered tombs and at the Er-Lannic stone circle. Aubrey Burl suggests that an intrusive Breton aristocracy may have been involved at this stage. By this time Stonehenge also had approximate astronomical alignments on midsummer sunrise and midwinter sunset.

In Phase 3iii the bluestones were brought back and set in a circle within the sarsen monument. This design seems to have been short-lived because in Phase 3iv they were repositioned to form a circle and an oval. After minor alterations Phase 3v became the sarsen circle and bluestone horseshoe setting that we know today. At some point during Phase 3 a parallel-sided banked and ditched Avenue was constructed, leading from the north-east entrance of Stonehenge for 2.8 km to the river Avon, close to modern Amesbury. The final period of construction was Phase 3vi, when two concentric rings of pits known as the Y and Z holes were dug outside the sarsen circle. They do not appear to have ever held stones or posts and they may represent an abandoned project.

Phase 3 of Stonehenge lasted a thousand years, from the time of the grooved ware users and the makers of beaker pots to the rich Wessex chieftains of the middle bronze age. Many changes of beliefs, ideas and uses are probably reflected in the numerous alterations to the monument, culminating in the building around the Stonehenge skyline of cemeteries of rich Wessex culture barrows. By then it must have become the focus of ritual in an otherwise agrarian landscape: a concept difficult to imagine unless we invoke the cautious analogy of the varied fortunes of the great Christian cathedrals, like Salisbury and Ely, which have also dominated the countryside for a thousand years.

Clearly linked to the henge monuments are the first **stone circles** that were built in Britain. Usually more than 30 metres in diameter, they tend to be low-lying and to contain traces of fire and human bones, suggesting that they were used for some ceremonial purpose, possibly connected with human sacrifice. Often these neolithic rings have monoliths, single tall stones, standing a few metres outside the circle. It has been suggested that these line up with

34. The stone circle of Long Meg and Her Daughters (Cumbria), measuring 110 metres across, is the largest in northern England.

astronomical features, though this only occasionally seems to happen. Long Meg and Her Daughters in Cumbria is a good example (figure 34). The Daughters form the second largest stone circle in England, whilst the monolith Long Meg, viewed through the circle's entrance from its centre, aligns with midwinter sunset.

At Avebury in Wiltshire two small stone circles were constructed about 2800 BC. Two hundred years later a larger circle of a hundred sarsen stones was set up to enclose them. This in turn was surrounded by a massive bank and internal ditch broken by

35. An aerial view of the eastern sector of Avebury (Wiltshire) with its massive bank and internal ditch. Part of the great rings of sarsen stones is visible beyond the houses.

four entrances (figure 35). About 2400 BC two avenues of stones were laid out from Avebury: one, called the Kennet Avenue, led south to The Sanctuary, a circular wooden building surrounded by two circles of stones, on Overton Hill; the other, the Beckhampton Avenue, led to the west, but only one of its stones remains.

Timber circles were broadly contemporary with the stone circles (*c*.3000-1500 BC) and like them were usually freestanding, although, as observed above, they also occur as components of larger monuments. They may consist of single, double or multiple rings of posts and vary considerably in diameter from 7 metres at Moel-y-Gaer (Clwyd) to about 95 metres at East Stoke in Nottinghamshire. Freestanding timber circles include Oddendale (Cumbria), Sarn-y-bryn-caled (Powys) and Dorchester 3 (Oxfordshire), whilst The Sanctuary and Woodhenge (both Wiltshire) and Mount Pleasant (Dorset) are elements of more complex sites.

The great mound of Silbury Hill, just south of Avebury, also belongs to the late neolithic period. More than 150 metres in diameter and 40 metres high, it is surrounded by a ditch 37 metres wide. The first Silbury Hill was a round mound, about 36 metres in diameter, built of layers of turf and gravel, its edge perhaps retained by stakes, and surrounded by a broad deep ditch. Soon after construction the mound was enlarged to its present huge size with material from a new ditch. Though excavations failed to find a burial under Silbury, it still seems probable that it is an exceptionally large barrow. Others see it

36. Silbury Hill in Wiltshire is 40 metres high and was built in a number of stages, beginning about 2500 BC. It is probably a burial mound, although limited excavations have failed to find a burial chamber.

37. Beakers of necked and bell type found at Clifton and Kempston in Bedfordshire.

as a massive ceremonial platform. Radiocarbon samples from the mound suggest that it was begun around 2500 BC (figure 36).

Cremation seems to have been the most frequent method of burial for later neolithic people, although it was by no means exclusive. In the north of England cremations were placed in long barrows and round barrows. On Seamer Moor in North Yorkshire bodies were burnt on a platform before being covered by a long barrow. Elsewhere in Britain single unburnt inhumation burials with simple grave goods, covered by round barrows with enclosing ring-ditches, were quite common. The grave goods might reflect the status, occupation, wealth and dress of the deceased. They included leaf-shaped arrowheads, flint scrapers, polished stone axes (some of considerable size), antler mace heads, bone pins, jet belt fasteners, beads, and flat copper axes imported from Ireland.

THE BEAKER USERS
(2600 to 1600 BC)

By 2600 BC entirely new items began to find their way into single-grave burials. Foremost were finely made reddish general-purpose pots known as beakers (figure 37). Similar drinking vessels can be found intermittently across western Europe from Norway and Hungary to Morocco, Portugal and Ireland. In Britain the first beakers were bell-shaped and decorated with cord impressions. Regional variations can be recognised and for a century and a half attempts have been made to demonstrate a typological and chronological sequence in which the original bell-shaped vessel later devel-

62

38. A bell beaker with twisted-cord decoration, a stone wristguard, a flint arrowhead and a copper tanged dagger from a bowl-barrow on Roundway Down (Wiltshire).

oped a short neck before finally becoming long-necked. Now radiocarbon dating of material associated with the beakers suggests that most of the styles were broadly contemporary and in use between 2600 BC and 1600 BC. Although frequently found with burials, there is little doubt that beakers were primarily made for domestic purposes.

Most beakers are decorated all over the exterior, and sometimes inside the necks as well, with horizontal lines made by impressing two-strand twisted cord into the wet fabric. This gives them their alternative name of all-over-cord (AOC) beakers. In Wessex decoration with a comb or toothed wheel was popular. It is doubtful if such beakers would have appeared in Britain if there had not been close contact with the continent, particularly the Netherlands. It is possible that their appearance was the result of small-scale invasions, although it is more usual to suggest that some were received initially as gifts, and the majority were copied locally in Britain and represent fashionable symbols of prestige, worthy of use in the home and the tomb. In many cases they occur in graves with other new and acceptable exotic types of grave goods, such as barbed-and-tanged arrowheads, wristguards, shale and jet buttons and beads, tanged triangular copper daggers and knives, awls and pins, and a few simple gold objects such as basket earrings and button cappings (figure 38). Graves containing weapons were exclusively male, and those with beads for women or children. Perishable items like clothing, food and floral tributes have seldom been recorded.

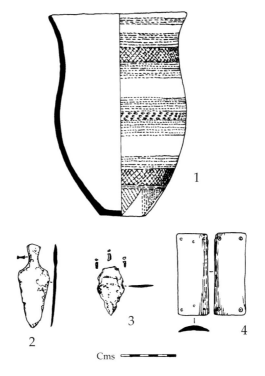

39. A fine bell-shaped beaker (1), together with a tanged bronze dagger (2), a triangular copper knife with three rivets to secure its hilt (3) and an archer's wristguard (4), found with the crouched burial of a man at Dorchester-on-Thames, Oxfordshire.

The majority of beaker burials occurred under round barrows and ring-cairns (in western Britain), but it was not unusual for them also to be placed in existing long barrows (Thickthorn Down) and the upper filling of causewayed enclosure ditches and henge monuments.

Makers of beakers buried the dead singly, in a crouched-up position, resembling a sleeping posture or the unborn foetus, under a burial mound. Barrows covering long-necked beaker burials are noticeably larger than those over bell-beakers. Men, women and children might be buried with beakers, and as time passed the same mound might act as a focus for further interments.

A burial from Roundway Down in Wiltshire contained the skeleton of a man with a bell-beaker, a copper knife-dagger about 25 cm long, a V-perforated button made of shale or jet, a barbed-and-tanged arrowhead, an archer's wristguard and a copper pin. This was a rather lavish collection and many graves contain only a

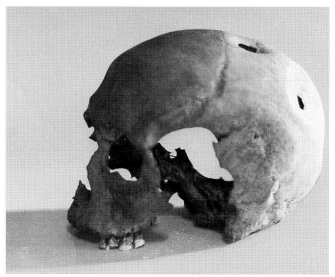

40. This beaker period skull shows the results of two successful attempts at brain surgery.

burial and a beaker (figure 39).

The objects from the Roundway Down grave throw some light on the daily routine of the beaker users, including their social life and craft activities. We know that they wore clothes of woven woollen fabrics, as well as animal skins, which could be fixed with buttons or with pins. Their hair may have been held in place with copper pins. They hunted with copper knives and bows and arrows and protected their wrists from the recoil of the bowstring with wristguards. From their beakers they probably drank water, milk or some alcoholic brew like mead made from lime honey and barley, which we know they grew. Differences of wealth and social status are demonstrated by the varying richness of grave goods; gold discs have been found and it is perhaps possible in some of the beaker graves to see the beginnings of a warrior aristocracy, though there is no direct evidence for warfare. These graves also contain so-called stone battleaxes with shaft-holes for the attachment of a wooden handle.

Among the most remarkable feats of prehistory are attempts at **trepanation** (brain surgery), noticed for the first time in the beaker graves. By cutting a roundel of bone from the skull with a flint knife it was probably believed that evil spirits could be released, so curing epilepsy, convulsions, madness and severe headaches (figure 40). It is even more remarkable that some people survived the operation in view of the possibilities of infection, haemorrhage and shock. We know that one person survived until the fourth attempt!

Few distinctive beaker settlements or earthworks have been found in Britain. About two dozen houses are known and extensive occupation debris has often been found. At Belle Tout, near Beachy Head in East Sussex, three different types of houses, two with oval plans and one rectangular, have been found associated with rectangular earthwork enclosures.

It may have been the beaker users who discovered rich copper deposits in Ireland and learnt to manufacture simple flat axes from them. They certainly introduced these axes into Britain, following a well-marked trade route along the south coast of Wales. The earliest Irish evidence comes from copper mines at Ross Island, Killarney, and dates between 2400 and 2000 BC. Another important Irish site, Mount Gabriel (County Cork), was worked between 1700 and 1400 BC. Of twenty known mining locations in Wales, the most extensive so far investigated is at Great Orme, near Llandudno, and was in use between 1700 and 700 BC. This spectacular mining complex seems to have been one of the largest in Europe (figure 41).

Towards the end of the third millennium BC there were further developments in three of the types of monument already known in Britain, namely stone circles, stone rows and henges. We still know very little about **stone circles**, although it is clear that like henges they are essentially a British development. Detailed study

41. The entrance to the bronze age copper mines on Great Orme Head near Llandudno in north Wales. An extensive network of tunnels followed veins of copper ore deep into the limestone.

by Alexander Thom showed that many were planned with geometric precision, some in eastern Scotland using a localised unit of length possibly based on a normal human pace, called by Thom a megalithic yard (0.83 metre). Whilst some of the stone circles are often true circles, others are egg-shaped, ellipses and what Thom called 'flattened circles'. It is clear that many of them seem to be aligned on the rising or setting sun or moon at the solstices. Thus they were probably set up to record astronomical observations, perhaps linked to significant events in the life of their builders, particularly periods in the farming year. Such a link between astronomy and crop and animal fertility may have resulted in semi-religious ceremonies being performed within the circles. Some of the circles were very large. At Stanton Drew in Somerset the Great Circle was 112.2 metres in diameter. Others, like the Rollright Stones in Oxfordshire and the Hurlers in Cornwall, were much smaller. All of them seem to have less association with human remains by this time, although the idea was still prevalent in Scotland. Many twelve-stone circles were set up in Cumbria (figure 42). In Wales the circles were also small, but two on Trecastle Mountain and Cerrig Duon (Powys), Gors Fawr (Pembrokeshire) and Druid's Circle in Gwynedd are all worth a visit. There are about ninety small stone circles on Dartmoor, with larger ones at the edges, as well as sixty short **stone rows**. The rows often lead up

42. The tiny 'four-poster' Goatstones stone circle near Simonburn in Cumbria. There are thirteen cup-marks on the left-hand stone.

to the circles. Good examples can be seen at Merrivale, some 7.2 km east of Tavistock, and at Drizzlecombe near Yelverton (Devon). Many of the smaller circles may have been kerbs around the edges of destroyed burial mounds.

Mount Pleasant, a large 4.45 hectare henge earthwork enclosure to the east of Dorchester (Dorset), had a smaller henge within it, which once contained five concentric rings of posts. It seems unlikely that this was ever a roofed building as has sometimes been suggested. The posts were later replaced by a central rectangular 'cove' of standing stones. About 2100 BC a massive timber palisade enclosing 4.05 hectares was built by beaker users inside the main enclosure. It was constructed of some 1600 oak posts, each standing about 6 metres above ground level and 50 cm in diameter. At the north and east entrances enormous posts 1.5 metres in diameter flanked extremely narrow gates. The palisade would have been most effective in preventing anyone from observing ceremonies being enacted within the sacred enclosure. Similar palisaded enclosures are known at West Kennet near Avebury (Wiltshire), Greyhound Yard, Dorchester (Dorset), and Hindwell near Knighton (Powys).

Arbor Low and the Bull Ring in Derbyshire were both henge monuments containing stone circles, although the stones from the Bull Ring were removed in the nineteenth century. Further fine circles can be seen at Swinside and Castlerigg in Cumbria.

THE BRONZE AGE
(early, 2200-1750 BC; middle, 1750-1000 BC; late, 1000-800 BC)
During the later neolithic and early bronze age the climate was drier than today, with long warm summers. In southern Britain substantial areas of forest had been cleared so that cereal crops might be grown on the lighter lowland soils, and sheep and cattle could graze close to watering places as well as on open downland. The earlier exploitation of natural resources for food continued and included a wide variety of roots, berries and leaves. Many fish, birds and wild animals were hunted, either with slings, wooden spears or bows and arrows, the last fitted with barbed-and-tanged flint arrowheads.

Our knowledge of domestic settlements in the early bronze age is rather sparse. Small farmsteads constructed largely of wood and daubed clay have left little trace in the countryside: postholes and rubbish pits are usually the only constructional clues that survive. Whilst some were single isolated homesteads, others were grouped to form hamlets of less than a dozen buildings that included dwellings, byres, store and work huts. Sometimes a surrounding ditch and bank, perhaps faced with a palisade or crowned by a

43. Ancient droveways were marked by V-shaped ditches separating small square fields at Fengate near Peterborough.

thorn hedge, served to keep out wild animals and contain domestic stock and wandering children. Extensive excavations at Fengate, on the outskirts of Peterborough (Cambridgeshire), revealed a system of early bronze age droveways, defined by V-shaped parallel ditches running between rectangular fields (figure 43). Gates strategically placed in the field corners made for easy movement of cattle to fen-edge grazing. A round house some 8 metres in diameter, with a central hearth and a porch on its eastern side, had stood in one paddock. Rain falling on to its thatched roof would have drained into an eaves-drip gulley, from where it could have run into the drove ditch or been collected for domestic purposes. Drinking water was also obtained for animals and man by digging shallow watering holes or 'sock' wells.

On the moors of western Britain circular stone dwellings were in existence by the early bronze age and continued to be built for many centuries. At Shaugh Moor on Dartmoor five circular stone houses were ranged around the inside of a stone-walled enclosure. Thirty-two saddle querns found at the site show that grain was being ground, but its position on a north-facing slope suggests that its activities were more probably pastoral rather than arable. The presence of a number of whetstones indicates that metal tools were in use, but there was no evidence to show that the settlement had any direct connection with the metallurgical trade of the area.

Throughout most of the bronze age **round barrows**, already common during the neolithic period, proliferate into extensive cemeteries. They tend to spread out in lines from, or cluster around, one particular burial mound, which probably contained the remains of a revered ancestor. This might be a long barrow as in the group at Winterbourne Stoke to the west of Stonehenge, or the round barrow containing a neolithic cremation at the centre of the Snail Down necropolis near Everleigh in Wiltshire (figure 44). During the second millennium BC cremation slowly replaced inhumation (unburnt) burials. The funeral ceremonies were almost certainly long and elaborate. The corpse may have lain in state for some time before burial, often long enough for the flesh to decay. Perhaps shamans or astrologers were called upon to determine the most propitious time for burial. The corpse was then laid on a funeral pyre and burnt. The bones were washed to remove any ashes and taken to the burial site in collared urns or wooden boxes, or tied up in a cloth or leather bag. A funeral feast would have been held outside the sacred area, probably accompanied by singing and dancing. The burial deposit would then be placed in a small pit at the centre of the site and perhaps a miniature wooden hut would be built above it. Some days later the barrow mound would be constructed from turves and from earth dug from an encircling ditch. Baskets of soil might be brought from some distance, perhaps indicating the extent of the territories with which the dead person

44. Two bell-barrows on Ministry of Defence land at Snail Down near Everleigh in Wiltshire. They have been damaged by tank activity.

had connections. A ring of posts, lintelled together, might be placed round the barrow to delimit the territory of the dead. Quite complicated burial rites of this type can be reconstructed from painstaking modern excavations.

In 1994 at Lockington in north-west Leicestershire a small pit was found just outside the encircling ditch of a cremation barrow. Inside it were two fine gold armlets, two pottery vessels (a crude beaker and a collared urn) and a copper dagger. They can be dated to the early bronze age. We are left with the question 'Were these gifts for the recent dead or for the ancestors, or was there some intention of recovering them at a later date?'

A similar burial sequence was observed when the body was not cremated (inhumation). In that case the corpse might be placed in a wooden coffin, a hollowed tree-trunk, a wicker basket or a woollen shroud. A number of bodies were still buried in a crouched or flexed position. Normally a barrow covered only one cremation or inhumation of a man, woman or child. This is called the **primary burial**, but other corpses were sometimes buried at the same time (**satellite burials**), and these may have been human sacrifices – servants or members of a family, perhaps, dying with a person of importance. In two barrows at Dunstable (Bedfordshire) large central graves containing single corpses were surrounded by rings of six and seven smaller contemporary graves. It seems certain that only a select few were buried in round barrows, but who they were or why they were chosen is not clear. Some of the earlier barrows seem to have been reopened at irregular intervals to accommodate further (**secondary**) burials, as at Duggleby Howe and Quernhow (Yorkshire) and Letch Farm (Hampshire). Barrows retained their sanctity for hundreds of years and were perhaps seen in folk memory as the last resting places of legendary and heroic ancestors. Centuries later, new burials could be added to the mound, which at the same time might be enlarged.

Soon after 2000 BC major changes took place in the area we call Wessex. This is roughly where the main hill ridges of southern England converge on Salisbury Plain. For centuries trackways had followed these hills and Wessex had become a route centre of some importance. Rivers also provided entry to the area, and its proximity to the south coast made it easily accessible both to and from Brittany and the continent. A few small agricultural communities living in Wessex acquired material wealth, not only by farming efficiently, but possibly by developing a skilful system of exchange and barter, and perhaps operating some form of control over the use of the ridgeways. This eventually led to the creation of a stratified society of chieftain-farmers who dominated their neighbours.

By this time the knowledge that a tough new metal called bronze could be made by mixing together 90 per cent copper and 10 per cent tin had reached Britain. Some of the farmers' kinsmen probably travelled in Europe, where they not only acquired tools and weapons made of bronze but also learnt how metal-bearing rock formations might be recognised, and the techniques of metal production. On their return to Britain they began prospecting for ores in Wales and the south-west in order to make their own copies of European products, including daggers, spears and pins. An area like St Just in Cornwall would have been an ideal place, with copper and tin ores occurring naturally together. In southern Europe demands for metal ores were exceeding supply and it seems likely that in due course Cornish and Welsh ores were exported to the continent.

It is likely that the canny Wessex chieftains were able to direct some of this trade through their territory. Acting in the lucrative role of middlemen, they would have been able to demand tolls and acquire for themselves not only personal wealth but also a share of exotic commodities from the Baltic, northern Germany, Brittany and perhaps even the Near East. This may have contributed towards the creation of the tiered structure of society in Wessex mentioned above, with groups of aristocratic land-owning chieftains and their ladies at the top and linked together through lineage, supported by a warrior class below them and at the bottom the poorer working folk.

A picture such as this is suggested by considering the contents of about a hundred rich graves found under cemeteries of round barrows, largely, though not exclusively, confined to the Wessex region (figure 45). Arranged in rows or nucleated groups, these 'Wessex' burial mounds varied in architectural styles. Men were usually buried in bell-barrows – large mounds of earth separated by a wide flat space from a surrounding ditch and outer bank. The richer women were buried under the tiny mounds of disc-barrows. Other Wessex barrows included saucer-barrows (low mounds of earth surrounded by a ditch normally covering female burials, although they occasionally contained men) and bowl-barrows, the simplest barrows of all, each consisting of a mound of earth, with or without a surrounding ditch, covering burials of both sexes. Also found in barrow groups are pond-barrows, which are shallow circular hollows with banks around them. Small pits in the floors of pond-barrows sometimes contain cremations and sometimes are empty: they were possibly originally intended for libations.

Amongst a variety of rich objects buried in these Wessex graves were necklaces and pendants of Baltic amber, flint axes from Scandinavia, stone battleaxes and decorative pins from northern

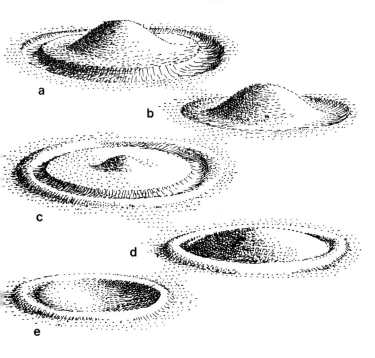

45. The most common types of round barrow found in southern Britain: (from top to bottom) bell, bowl, disc, saucer and pond.

Germany and ceremonial jadeite axes from Brittany. The craftsmen of southern England also became adept at fashioning rich objects of their own: for example, a gold cup found at Rillaton in Cornwall (figure 46) and part of another from Cuxwold in Lincolnshire, amber cups from Hove (East Sussex) and Winterbourne St Martin (Dorset), a gold cape from Mold (Clwyd) and gold-bound amber discs from various places. The grave of a man buried beneath Bush Barrow, to the south of Stonehenge, contained sheet-gold body ornaments, a bronze axe, a stone mace head and three daggers, one with fine gold-nail inlay decoration on its hilt (figure 47). Apart from the exotic objects already mentioned, men's graves often contained bronze axes, and daggers with a rib down their centre and grooves at the edge of the blade. Women might be

46. A tiny gold cup, 8.2 cm high, from a Wessex-type burial at Rillaton in Cornwall.

47. A dagger from Bush Barrow, to the south of Stonehenge, with fine gold-nail inlay on the hilt.

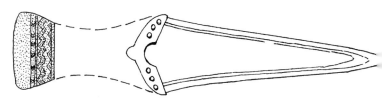

48. A collared urn decorated with twisted-cord impressions, and a grape cup or incense cup, from a bowl-barrow at Wilsford near Stonehenge.

buried with crescent-shaped necklaces of amber or shale and little enigmatic pottery vessels of various designs, rather dubiously named incense cups (figure 48).

Pottery found in graves of the early bronze age ranges from late beakers and food vessels to collared, cordoned and encrusted urns. Many of these vessels were contemporaneous, though some appear more frequently in one region than another. It is not unusual to find a beaker and a food vessel in the same barrow, though the beaker is usually in the pre-eminent position at the centre of the mound, whilst the food vessel tends to occupy a secondary or satellite position. The food-vessel occurred only in a primary position when the beakers had ceased to be fashionable by about 1600 BC. The urn users sometimes built their own barrows, but they were quite happy to make use of any pre-existing mound as a burying place for their cremations.

The so-called **food vessels** are vase- or bowl-shaped pots, often heavily decorated, which have evolved from, and replace, late

49. A food-vessel and collared urn of the early bronze age. The collared urn is about 30 cm high.

neolithic pottery forms and beakers (figure 49). The vase-shaped urns tend to occur in England, particularly in the north, whilst the bowls are found in Ireland and a mixture of both occurs in Scotland. The food vessels are found in both inhumation and cremation graves. Crescentic jet necklaces, like the Wessex amber examples, are a feature of the food-vessel graves in Yorkshire, Derbyshire and Scotland.

Collared urns are distributed throughout the British Isles. Like food vessels, they seem to have begun by 2000 BC and, whilst they were often later used for domestic purposes, they were primarily containers for cremations, which became popular about that time. South of the Pennines they are usually buried singly or in groups under a barrow, whilst in northern Britain they tend to occur in flat cemeteries. Both collared urns and food vessels passed out of fashion around 1400 BC.

Some of the most interesting bronze age burials in Yorkshire were found in oak coffins. One of the best-preserved examples came from Gristhorpe, on the coast between Scarborough and Filey. The coffin had been made by splitting an oak trunk in half and gouging out the inside. It had been placed beneath a barrow at the bottom of a pit dug into waterlogged boulder clay. Inside was the skeleton of a tall, well-built man. His body had been wrapped in an animal skin, fastened at the chest with a bone pin. A bronze knife with a whalebone pommel had been buried with him. The coffin is now in the Scarborough Museum. Another tree-trunk burial was found in a barrow called Loose Howe, which lies 8 km south of Danby, high on the North York Moors. It, too, had been preserved by waterlogging, although most of the contents had disappeared. Part of a left shoe and foot wrappings survived, together with a bronze knife. Lying preserved beside the Loose Howe coffin was a 2.7 metres long dugout canoe with a beak-like prow, reminding us of the importance of river transport. Tree-trunk coffins are also known from barrows in Wessex and Wales.

In the north and west of Britain barrows were often constructed of stones, the ditch of the south sometimes being replaced by retaining kerbs or dry-stone walls. Stone-built barrows are fre-

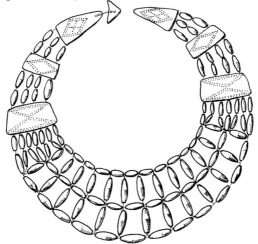

50. *A crescentic jet necklace of the type worn by women in the north of England.*

quently called **cairns**. In the centre stone slabs might be used to form a **cist**, this in essence being nothing more than a stone coffin for the body. Although burials were individual, a number of cists might occur under one barrow. Some of the stone cist slabs have cup-and-ring marks on them, emphasising the religious or super-stitious nature of the carvings. It is possible, however, that some of the decorated slabs may have been reused.

Inhumation burials give us clues about the clothes people wore in the bronze age. Buttons and pins have often survived in graves, and in Denmark actual woollen fabrics have been preserved in waterlogged soil. These show that some men wore long woollen skirts or kilts which were high enough to cover the chest, had shoulder straps and were tied at the waist. Poncho-type capes and close-fitting hemispherical woollen caps were also worn. Jet buttons found near a man's feet in Yorkshire suggest that he may have worn gaiters or leggings that buttoned at the ankles. Trousers do not seem to have been in fashion until horse-riding became popular around 1000 BC. Women wore long woollen dresses with half-length sleeves in the winter, and square-necked jumpers and corded skirts during the warmer summer months. A woven belt kept the skirt in position. The hair was covered with a net or cap, or held in place with long bone or jet pins. Items of jewellery such as gold earrings and jet ear studs, together with small domestic knives and awls, are often found in women's graves (figure 50), whilst men are more frequently accompanied by battleaxes, arrowheads and larger knives.

By 1600 BC the wealth of Wessex had declined. New centres of bronze metalworking in eastern and south-eastern England had already emerged, known as the **Arreton** industry, which included cast-flanged axes, ogival daggers, tanged spearheads and socketed pegged spearheads. Objects of flint and igneous rocks, which had been so important even in the early bronze age, now ceased to be produced, as did the whole range of pottery types like food vessels, collared urns and incense cups. Although barrow burial and cremation survived, everything else connected with the religious life of the earlier periods was abandoned, although the sites were still respected – the stone circles and alignments, the henges and the cursuses; and, perhaps rather surprisingly, the remarkable astronomical information and its associated mathematics seem to have been forgotten also.

It is difficult to suggest reasons for what looks like a period of economic decline. Colin Burgess has drawn attention to the onset of a climatic deterioration which might have begun around 1200 BC. It is just possible that a worsening climate resulting in flooding and waterlogging could have caused the abandonment of the old sky gods for new water gods, resulting in the discarding of many old beliefs and the introduction of new ones, including the depositing of quality bronze offerings in the fens and rivers of south-eastern England.

A new group of pottery forms characterised by coarse urns of barrel, bucket and globular types, and for convenience given the all-embracing name of **Deverel-Rimbury**, became the standard vessels of the middle bronze age (1400-1000 BC). Distinctive regional groups of urns emerge, particularly in southern England, whilst only the bucket urns are widely distributed throughout Britain. Most of the urns were decorated with fingertips and bands of applied clay. They were used as containers for cremations as well as for domestic purposes.

Eventually burial beneath round barrows declined in use, and cremation became more popular. The ashes were placed in urns and buried in flat cemeteries or inserted into or around existing earlier barrows. Grave goods were very rare. At Simons Ground (Dorset) more than three hundred cremations were deposited in small urnfields on the southern side of a group of barrows, over a period of nearly six hundred years, starting about 1250 BC. There is evidence for strong contacts with the Low Countries between 1300 and 1100 BC. Biconical cremation urns made in southern and eastern England are identical to Hilversum urns from the Netherlands, and metalwork is almost indistinguishable on either side of the Channel.

Farming was of prime importance in southern Britain. Small circular farm huts were surrounded by wooden stockades for protection against wild animals and connected by trackways to rectangular **fields**, which are misleadingly called 'Celtic'. These fields varied in size up to about 0.4 hectare and might cover 5 square km. They were used primarily for growing barley, which was cut with short-handled sickles with metal blades. Grain storage pits in Hut 3 at Black Patch (East Sussex) contained 56 kg of carbonised barley. Other cereals, legumes and brassicas were also grown. Most farms reserved much larger areas of downland for grazing cattle and goats, one 'ranch' often being separated from the next by deep V-shaped ditches with banks on which hedges were sometimes planted. Traces of these can still be seen on many uncultivated chalk downs. Horses may have been used for rounding up cattle. On the edge of the ranches woodland no doubt existed for foraging pigs. Farming units of this type would have housed twenty to thirty individuals – most likely extended families. Typical examples have been excavated at Thorny Down in Wiltshire and at Itford Hill and Plumpton Plain (both in Sussex), each with about a dozen huts. On the chalk downs at Black Patch, south-east of Lewes (East Sussex), is a flight of rectangular fields, some separated by hollow ways. These lead to hut platforms cut into the hillside. Excavation of one of the platforms revealed the postholes of five circular huts, some separated from each other by fences. The largest hut was about 10 metres in diameter with a conical thatched roof supported on oak posts and resting on the chalk hillside at the back and on low flint walls at the front. Evidence suggests that this was the headman's house, with the others either housing his wives, or used for food preparation, animal husbandry and storage.

On the high moors of western England and Wales, people also grew barley and herded sheep. Stone hut foundations and low rectangular walled enclosures indicate the development of a settled farming life, perhaps to some extent forced on the population

51. The footings of a small stone hut, about 2.5 metres in diameter, at Grimspound on Dartmoor. The pound wall, which encloses some twenty-four huts, runs across the picture.

by gradual climatic deterioration. It is in the highland parts of Britain that such buildings have survived. Low walls, circular in plan and a metre thick and high, sometimes with porches, supported timber rafters that rose to a point like a wigwam. **Hut circles** like this are scattered over Dartmoor; for example, at White Ridge, north of Postbridge, there are two groups of four and six huts respectively, each less than 6 metres in diameter, with small fields nearby for herds, flocks and crops. At Grimspound on Dartmoor is a walled stock enclosure containing twenty-four huts, some of which were used as storerooms by the herdsmen who lived there (figure 51). Above, the higher moorlands were probably common grazing lands. This rough land was separated from the settlement fields by regularly placed stone banks known as **reaves**. These seem to have been planned about 1300 BC as part of an enormous unified field system. More than 200 km of reaves can be traced across Dartmoor, enclosing about 10,000 hectares of better-quality land. Other stone huts have survived in Cornwall, Yorkshire, Cumbria, Northumberland and north-west Wales.

Not all bronze age houses were on the high moors. At Trevisker near St Eval in Cornwall two circular houses have been excavated on lower ground and were constructed of timber, though one was later rebuilt in stone. The inhabitants appear to have been engaged in metalworking as well as growing cereals. Close to a farmstead in a circular enclosure at Gwithian in Cornwall, the marks of cross-ploughing and spades have been found in eight small lyncheted fields that had been cultivated and manured over several seasons around 1300 BC. Even earlier plough marks have been found beneath a long barrow at South Street, near Avebury, which can be attributed to the early third millennium BC.

The remains of domesticated horses have been found dating back to beaker times, but we have no clear evidence that riding was established in Britain until the beginning of the first millennium. Riding horses were almost certainly a status symbol, made the more significant by the use of carved antler and fine bronze harness fittings. The value of horses would also have been appreciated in warfare, which is attested mainly by the proliferation of fortified enclosures at this time. In 1994 a new technique known as optical dating was applied to the Uffington White Horse, a stylised hill figure 110 metres long, cut into the chalk downland close to the Ridgeway in south Oxfordshire. Long believed to date from the late iron age, the new tests suggest that the horse was first dug into the hillside, perhaps as a tribal status emblem, in the late bronze age, around 1000 BC. It appears to have been kept clean and visible ever since. Wagons and carts had also made an appearance by 1000 BC. The earliest known cart wheel so far found in England is of plank construction. It measures 84 cm in diameter and was found in a waterlogged site at Flag Fen (Cambridgeshire). It is of comparable date to a disc wheel from Blair Drummond in Perthshire: around 1050 BC.

Metalworking techniques developed rapidly between the Arreton industry, which marked the end of the early bronze age, and an industrial revolution which was unleashed soon after 850 BC. Four overlapping stages of metalworking can be clearly seen, known chronologically as the Acton Park, Taunton, Penard and Wilburton-Wallington phases (figure 52). Thrusting rapiers gave way in the final phase (1000-750 BC) to slashing swords with leaf-shaped blades, protected by wooden sheaths. Broadly speaking, swords were the preferred weapon in northern Britain, spears in Wales and western England, and a mixture of both in south-east England. A new technique of bronze-casting, called the **lost wax** (*cire perdue*) method, was functioning. A model of the object to be fashioned was made in beeswax. This was then coated with clay and baked. The hot wax ran out and molten metal was poured into its place. When cool, the metal casting was the exact shape of the original model. A whole series of new and elaborate objects could now be mass-produced, thus making axes, sickles, weapons, harness and vehicle fittings available to all.

By 800 BC sheet metal was worked, too, and used to copy and improve on the design of cauldrons, buckets, shields and even trumpets that had arrived in Britain by way of trade or exchange from western Europe. At first the metal sheets were small and had

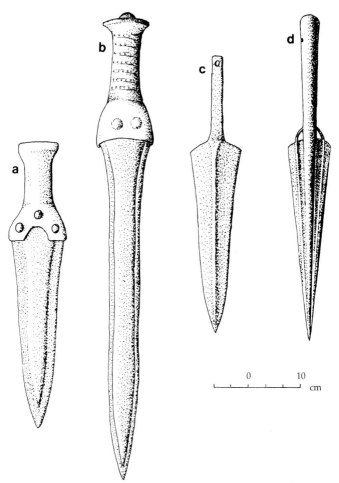

52. Examples of bronze age metalwork: a, an ogival dagger with three rivets; b, a dirk with metal hilt; c, a tanged spearhead; d, a basal-looped spearhead. (Rapiers shorter than 355 mm are termed dirks.)

to be riveted together. The introduction of cauldrons brought with it the ability to boil large quantities of food, hitherto prohibited by the lack of a suitable container.

Itinerant metalfounders or tinkers moving from farm to farm collected old and broken bronzes, which could be melted down and reused many times. Occasionally they buried these for collection later and, when they failed to retrieve them, they remained undetected until modern times. These collections are known as **found-**

ers' hoards. The Isleham hoard (Cambridgeshire) was found in 1959. It consisted of more than 6500 fragments of bronze that had been buried in a small pit. As well as broken weapons and ornaments, there were harness fittings and cauldron fragments. Other metal hoards were the result of **votive deposition**. Fine-quality weapons, ceremonial objects and ornaments, often accompanied by animal remains, have been found in rivers, lakes and marshes, where they seem to have been deliberately placed to placate the water gods.

The late bronze age closes with the appearance of the Ewart Park phase of metalworking, described as an industrial revolution due to the sudden surge in metal productivity and the appearance of new and sometimes exotic items. This may be partly the result of the first indications of unsettled conditions in central Europe, heralding the spread of Celtic power. A great increase in bronze spearheads suggests that the population was ready to defend itself, as well as continuing to hunt in the still extensive forests.

Between 1000 and 500 BC there was a marked deterioration in the climate, conditions becoming cooler and wetter than in the previous, comparatively warm and dry period, and the mean temperature dropped by 2°C. The change was more keenly felt in the uplands of northern Britain, where land once settled and cultivated was abandoned or turned over to rough pasture.

Soon after 1200 BC wooden palisades and sometimes bank and ditch enclosures were being erected on a few hilltops in central southern England. While some of these defences have been identified as pastoral enclosures, a number already exhibit more strength and strategic siting than seems necessary for ordinary agricultural purposes. Norton Fitzwarren (Somerset), Harrow Hill (West Sussex), Rams Hill (Oxfordshire) and others have been variously interpreted as trading centres and communal meeting places, though they may represent nothing more than a response to the developing need for security caused by cattle raiding and localised skirmishes. Here the origins of the hillforts probably lie; and before the end of the bronze age examples with strong timbered box-ramparts were already functioning at sites like Grimthorpe in Yorkshire, The Breiddin (Powys), Dinorben (Clwyd) and Ivinghoe Beacon in Buckinghamshire.

In eastern England a group of more than sixteen circular ditched enclosures have been recognised, usually 50 to 100 metres in diameter, containing one or more large circular houses. The distinctive quality of their construction has led to the suggestion that they were the headquarters of local chieftains. Excavated examples dated between 1100 and 800 BC include Mucking and Springfield Lyons in Essex and Thwing in Yorkshire.

At Runnymede Bridge, Egham (Surrey), a well-preserved trading settlement site has been excavated beside the river Thames. Oak piles had been driven into the riverbank for more than 35 metres to provide a quay for river traffic. The settlement, which ran back 100 metres from the waterfront, was closely packed with buildings, where weaving, flint and metal working and probably pottery making were all practised. The inhabitants seem to have been pastoralists in view of the large numbers of cattle, sheep and pig bones found.

Three unusual late bronze age to early iron age sites have been found in Wiltshire at Potterne, Blagdon Hill and East Chisenbury. Successive 'villages' of timber buildings seem to have been constructed on the same site, each covered with layers of rubbish, which formed into vast middens, like the tells of the Middle East. These middens may be up to 3 metres thick and 4-5 hectares in extent. That at Potterne seemed to be composed of vast quantities of horse manure, and they all contained many fragments of quality pottery and semi-exotic ornaments, as well as discarded metal tools and animal bones.

THE PRE-ROMAN IRON AGE: EARLY PHASE
(800 to 450 BC)

Life in early iron age Britain continued much as it had done in the late bronze age. There was no clear break between the two, but as time went on rapid changes in pottery and metal styles indicate strong influences from the continent, where there were great movements of Celtic population. There is no positive evidence to suggest that any large-scale folk movements reached Britain, but from time to time a few small groups of adventurers may have settled on the coasts. They need not necessarily have left traces that would have made any marked impression on the archaeological record. Pottery of the fifth and fourth centuries BC found along the seaboard of northern France and the Low Countries so closely matches vessels found in Sussex, Kent and East Anglia that one cannot totally rule out the possibility of immigrant settlers.

Soon after 450 BC small bands of people do seem to have moved into south-east Yorkshire from northern France. They were an offshoot of the Gaulish tribe known as the Parisii; in Britain they are known as the **Arras culture**, after the East Yorkshire village where one of their richest cemeteries has been found. They stand out from the other iron age people because of their method of burial. Their commoners were buried in simple interments under small barrows, their graves containing few personal ornaments. In more than a dozen graves of their leaders, who might be either men or women, were found complete or dismantled two-wheeled carts that had been used as funeral hearses. In a woman's grave were a bronze mirror, a gold and iron pin decorated with coral, and a horse bridle. Men were buried with their horses and shields. Most of the

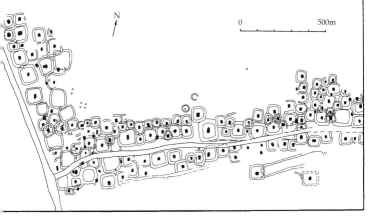

53. Part of the linear cemetery of square Arras culture graves excavated at Wetwang Slack (East Yorkshire). (After J. S. Dent.)

graves had contained joints of pork. The burial mounds themselves were surrounded by ditches forming a square. More than five hundred Arras culture barrows are known from Burton Fleming (see figure 6), and almost as many at Danes' Graves, near Driffield. A linear cemetery, revealed by aerial photography at Wetwang Slack, ran for more than 1 km beside a prehistoric trackway (figure 53). The excavators uncovered 446 burials, more than two hundred of which were enclosed by square barrow ditches. There is no doubt that a lot of the ornaments in the Arras graves were family heirlooms that came directly from the continent, though the carts and harness fittings were later British copies.

With the exception of a dozen stone-cist cemeteries in south-west England (similar to ones found in Brittany), evidence for burial in the rest of iron age Britain is almost non-existent until the first century BC. For something like six hundred years there are no inhumation or cremation cemeteries. It seems probable that, as in the neolithic period, bodies were excarnated – perhaps placed on four-post platforms and exposed to the ravages of nature: the weather and carnivorous animals and birds. Afterwards the bones might be collected up and used for ancestor worship, or even crushed and used as medicine! Odd human bones are often found on habitation sites. Alternatively corpses might have been cremated and the ashes scattered over the fields or in pools, rivers or sacred groves. Of course excarnation and cremation could naturally have followed each other.

Many trading and exchange contacts existed which enabled continental inventions and fashions to be seen and copied in Britain,

54. The excavation of an iron age roundhouse at Salford Quarry (Bedfordshire). The inner circle represents the footing trench of the house, the outer circle the roof-drip gulley. The entrance porch was in the foreground.

producing a sort of second-hand or native Celtic culture. Classical texts record the exchange of tin between Mediterranean traders and the occupants of *Belerium* (the Penwith peninsula of Cornwall).

Throughout the iron age the climate in southern Britain was cool and wet and agriculture continued to form the basis of life. Small **farmsteads** existed widely across the country. The farmhouse was a circular building constructed of different regional materials and varying in size; for example, at Little Woodbury in Wiltshire it was 15 metres in diameter and at Gill Mill, Ducklington (Oxfordshire), only 8 metres. Such house types survived for hundreds of years. One or more central posts, surrounded by a ring of smaller posts, often supported a wide conical roof (figure 54). The walls were usually of wattle daubed with clay, or a continuous circle of posts set in a palisade trench. Smoke from a central hearth escaped through a hole in the roof, whilst a porch may have given added protection from draughts and driving rain at the door. The same sort of house, translated into stone, existed in the highland part of Britain and clearly continued the house styles of the bronze age. Walled villages reminiscent of Grimspound occur in a more compact form during the iron age at places like Bodrifty in Cornwall. There, a strong stone wall enclosed around 1.5 hectares and contained eight huts which varied in diameter between 9 and 14 metres. Another enclosed village of about twenty huts, ranging in size from 2.4 to 6 metres in diameter, can be seen at Greaves Ash in Northumberland.

Whilst some of the lowland farms were undefended, others were surrounded by a palisade or bank with an external ditch; this offered protection from wild animals and contained the domestic herds and children. Extensive excavations on the river gravels of Oxfordshire show that mixed farming took place on the higher terraces of rivers like the Windrush. More specialised farms were established on the lower terraces and flood plains, where intensive cattle and horse rearing took place. Economically, surplus grain and horses may have been exchanged for Derbyshire quernstones,

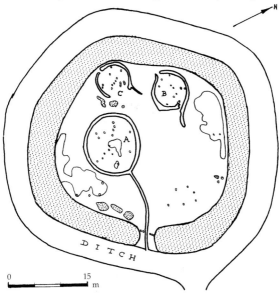

55. A defended early iron age enclosure at Draughton (Northamptonshire). The three huts (A, B and C) have sumps leading from their footing trenches. The stippled bank is surrounded by an external ditch. (After W. F. Grimes.)

Droitwich salt and objects of shale, bronze and iron. Large numbers of pits for storing both dried and wet grain have been excavated in most south-eastern iron age settlements. However, in the highland zone, west of a line drawn roughly from Bristol to Scarborough, grain-storage pits are lacking and we have to conclude that in that area the emphasis must have been on raising flocks and herds. At Draughton in Northamptonshire three circular huts were found in an enclosure only 30 metres in diameter (figure 55). The largest hut was 10.4 metres across, whilst the other two

56. Corn-grinding equipment: (left) a saddle quern and (right) a rotary quern.

were only 6 metres in diameter. In this case the excavator suggested that the settlement was occupied by a small group of ironworkers exploiting the local ironstone.

In the south **'Celtic' fields** on sloping downland continued to be cross-ploughed, and the introduction of a two-ox plough, together with some signs of soil exhaustion, made it possible and expedient to open up heavier valley soils. In the north spade and hoe cultivation continued in many places. Once it had been realised that farmyard manure helped land to remain fertile for long periods, it is probable that a two-field system of rotation was introduced, in which fields lay fallow in alternative years, so that they might be grazed and manured by the herds and flocks. As a rough guide a corn yield of about 25 bushels per hectare can be assumed in the iron age. That is roughly a third of the modern yield on chalk. Wheat tended to replace barley. Once the grain was gathered it was dried on a wooden rack and then parched in an oven to prevent it germinating, being then stored until it was required for grinding into flour; alternatively, grain required for planting in the following year was stored damp. Wet corn releases carbon dioxide which prevents the growth of bacteria, and experiments have shown that 75 per cent of the grain will germinate after a year's storage in underground storage pits. The wheat was ground by crushing the grain between the stones of either a **saddle quern**, the upper stone of which was rubbed backwards and forwards on the lower saddle-shaped stone, or from the second century BC onwards on a **rotary quern**, in which the upper stone revolved on the lower (figure 56).

Wool for clothing was produced all over Britain. Weaving must be regarded as a 'cottage' industry. Few farmhouses would have been without a vertical loom, and paired postholes in the hut floors may indicate their presence. Numerous triangular clay weights that kept the warp threads taut and the bone combs used to pack the weft tightly have been found. Roots and berries must have been used to dye the wool, which in texture would have resembled Harris tweed and was often likely to have been woven in chequered patterns.

57. Decorated cooking and storage vessels of the earlier iron age from All Cannings Cross (Wiltshire).

The men had a variety of jobs besides farming. Some worked as metalsmiths, wheelwrights, carpenters, tinkers and butchers, all needing and producing specialist tools like tongs, sickles, bill-hooks, gouges, files, awls, chisels and saws, each of which could be cheaply produced from wrought iron. Iron ores occur widely in Britain. For the huntsman the sling was the main weapon, although iron-headed spears, daggers and knives were available.

The women were responsible for weaving, cooking and making pots, which varied in design from one part of Britain to another. At first vessels were coarse and resembled the later bronze age urns. Their sides were often roughened to prevent them slipping from greasy hands. At meal times, finer wares were used, often with burnished surfaces, or decorated with curvilinear patterns (figure 57). Not all pottery was home-made, and localised regional types emerged. There is evidence that some of it was made in large quantities in the south-west and then distributed along the Jurassic Way through the Cotswolds as far as Leicestershire. Wooden dishes and bowls, again carved with fine patterns, took their place beside the clay vessels and tell us that man had discovered the use of the lathe.

There grew up in iron age Britain the beginnings of a form of feudal society. Some farmers, doing better than others, found it possible to employ labour, and so to become masters. Once dominant, these farmers took the lead in certain areas to become chieftains over what might ultimately be called a tribe. Initially petty jealousies doubtless broke out between one chieftain and another, and this was followed by fighting and plunder. From the late bronze age we find the more powerful of these petty chieftains setting up relatively simple defences: a single line of rampart and ditch ringing a hilltop to enclose about 5 hectares. Such sites, found particularly from central southern England to north Wales, are known as **hillforts**. It is not clear if the chieftains set up their houses inside the forts, whilst their tenants continued to farm outside. It seems most likely that the chieftains lived in the larger farmsteads like Little Woodbury and that everyone came into the fort to shelter with their herds and chattels when feuding and local wars broke out. Alternatively, cattle, which meant wealth, might be stalled in the fort at night for fear of cattle rustlers from a neighbouring fort. But this must be seen as an occasional threat and certainly not a permanent one.

THE PRE-ROMAN IRON AGE: MIDDLE PHASE
(450 to 100 BC)

During the middle iron age developed hillforts came into their own, and some of the earlier examples went out of use. In the majority of cases the essential feature of such structures was defence, and every effort was made to make them difficult to attack. Where natural features were inadequate, deep external ditches were dug, the material from them being piled into a stout timber and stone-faced rampart, set with a wooden stockade. By the second century BC the number of these artificial defences was to increase (**multivallate forts**), but initially single ramparts and ditches sufficed (**univallate forts**). A fort seldom had more than two entrances, since these were always a point of weakness and elaborate efforts were made to strengthen them. Wooden gates at angles to the ramparts, gates in inturned barbicans, gates protected by claw-like outworks, gates with footbridges for sentries over the top, all were tried with varying degrees of success. A glance at a plan of one of the entrances to Maiden Castle (Dorset) will demonstrate the lengths to which the builders carried their entrance designs (see figure 58).

In southern Britain hillforts were made as impregnable as possible by being sited on steep hilltops, the ramparts following the contours of the hill. Such earthworks are known as **contour forts** (Herefordshire Beacon, figure 59; Hambledon Hill, Dorset). In areas where no high hills existed or were unsuitable, the fort might

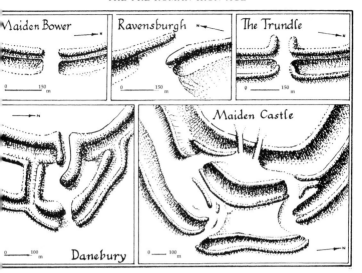

58. *Hillfort entrances: (above) simple type; (below) complex type.*

59. *The massive ramparts of the iron age contour hillfort on Herefordshire Beacon, near Malvern.*

be on lower ground. In that case the defences would be particularly strong; these are called lowland or **plateau forts** (Risbury, Herefordshire; Arbury Banks, Hertfordshire). If the sides of a hill spur were steep enough to afford natural defence, it might suffice to throw a line of rampart and ditch across the neck which joined the spur to the main hill mass. This resulted in a **promontory fort** (Boltby Scar, North Yorkshire; Bredon Hill, Worcestershire; Hengistbury Head, Dorset). The same method was employed on the coast of south-west England and Wales, where rocky headlands were cut off by one or more lines of defence to form **cliff castles** (Trevelgue Head, Cornwall; St David's Head, Pembrokeshire). Similar cliff castles are a slightly later feature on the headlands of Brittany and southern Ireland and show close cultural links with Britain. A group of non-defensive forts with widely spaced earthworks occurs on the sides of a number of hills in the West Country and occasionally elsewhere. Sometimes called multiple-enclosure or **hillslope forts**, they show evidence of lengthy human occupation. Their outer enclosures seem to have been used as cattle corrals and sheep pens (Milber Down and Clovelly Dykes, Devon; Goosehill, Sussex).

A few hillforts were unfinished (Ladle Hill, Hampshire; Elworthy, Somerset) and these give us some idea of how the earthworks were constructed. Shallow marking-out trenches first encircled the hilltop. These were followed by gangs of men digging deep ditches whilst others cut many hundreds of timbers for facing the rampart. Once the wooden posts were in position along the inner edge of the ditch, a second row of timbers was set about 3 metres behind them. The two rows were tied together with cross-timbers and the gap between was filled with turf and rubble. In stone country masons trimmed and laid dry-stone rampart facings as a substitute for, or sometimes in addition to, wood. The intricate work of building the entrances followed, often with guard chambers and sentry walks over the top. The average hillfort would need more than ten thousand timbers for its defences, and some of the larger ones would require many more. As there are about 1400 forts in England and Wales, the amount of forest clearance in the iron age must have been comparable with that of Elizabethan times.

It is clear that only a few hillforts were occupied permanently. Some chieftains may have wanted all their tenants living together for economic reasons; others preferred them close to the land in individual farmsteads. In many cases the fort served as a market and communal centre, occupied by only a token population 'out of trading hours'.

Hod Hill in Dorset contained more than two hundred circular houses within its ramparts (not necessarily all contemporary),

60. The complex eastern entrance to Danebury hillfort (Hampshire). Compare figure 58. It was destroyed by fire about 100 BC.

whilst the much smaller Conderton Camp (Worcestershire) produced evidence of a dozen large stone-built dwellings. In contrast Arbury Banks (Hertfordshire) in the Chilterns appears to hold a single large central house accompanied by a number of smaller farm buildings, and Figsbury Rings (Wiltshire) seems to have contained no buildings at all but to have served only as a cattle enclosure.

By the fourth century BC some of the developed hillforts such as Danebury (Hampshire) (figure 60) and Maiden Castle (Dorset) were like small towns, protected by prestigious defences, with streets lined by rows of houses that were frequently renewed, and three or four rectangular temples. In spite of this ostentation, the everyday material objects found in these forts are no different to those found in the rural settlements. At Danebury and at Croft Ambrey (Herefordshire) storage pits and rows of **four-post buildings**, each about 3 metres square, suggest that the forts were used as centralised storage depots for surplus grain, hides and wool. Their geographical position, such as close to the sea, or on the edge of tribal territories, may also have influenced the redistribution and exchange of commodities like salt, metal ores and perhaps pottery.

During the middle phase of the iron age, chieftains in the larger forts began to define their territories along the edges of forests, rivers and other natural features. Where these did not exist they constructed **dykes**, often with two or three deep ditches and high banks between. Their territories varied in size from a dozen to 60 square kilometres and have been recognised in many areas from

Wessex to the Yorkshire Wolds. The dykes sometimes cut across major trackways such as the Icknield Way, presumably to impede cattle rustlers and to make checks on population movements possible.

During the third century BC the **La Tène art style** was introduced into Britain. It had developed since the fifth century BC on the continent, from three main sources: geometric abstract designs, archaic oriental symbols, and classical botanical decoration. Under the patronage of aristocratic Celtic chieftains metalsmiths turned these ideas into 'a live source of artistic inspiration' (Paul Jocobsthal). In Britain these continental designs were seen and developed into an insular style which features flowing scrolls, tendrils and palmette designs, often highlighted in coloured enamel. One of the earliest examples of La Tène art in Britain is the cap of a horn, decorated with a tendril pattern and found in the Thames at Brentford (now in the Museum of London). Helmets, collars, buckles, scabbards, shields, bridle-bits, mirror-backs (figure 61) – on all of these until well into the first century AD the British craftsmen tried their skill, producing some of the most exciting art to come out of Europe since the cave artists. At the same time numerous exotic continental items found their way into Britain, particularly in the south-west, where there seems to have been a flourishing cultural exchange between Brittany, Cornwall, south Wales and southern Ireland.

61. The engraved back of a late pre-Roman iron age mirror from Old Warden (Bedfordshire).

THE PRE-ROMAN IRON AGE: LATE PHASE
(100 BC to AD 43)

From about 120 BC a large number of gold Gallo-Belgic coins appeared in southern Britain from Belgic Gaul and Armorica. They seem to have been brought into the country by small groups of influential Celtic immigrants and traders from northern Gaul and Brittany, before the arrival of a stronger influx of settlers who appeared in western Hampshire early in the first century BC and were known as the Belgae. These first coins were found around the Thames estuary from the Isle of Thanet to Essex and Colchester. They then spread on to the North Downs and into eastern Kent, as well as the central Chilterns.

The gold coins are probably best explained as gifts exchanged for goods or military service between the people of northern Gaul and a core of folk in south-east England. These two groups became culturally and economically very close with much movement between them. Not surprisingly, their pottery and burial customs were virtually identical. The British core group spread across Kent, Essex and Hertfordshire and is recognised by archaeologists as the **Aylesford-Swarling culture** (after two Kentish cemeteries). It is typified by cremation burials in pear-shaped pedestal urns placed in cemeteries of flat graves without covering barrows, and by bronze brooches of safety-pin type. Their Gaulish counterparts, referred to as the South Belgic culture, developed under Roman authority, between the Seine and the Rhine.

Quite early in the first century BC, using coin and ceramic evidence, it becomes possible to apply tribal names to sections of this British core group, which can then be divided into two politically distinct factions. South of the Thames the Atrebates and other native groups were minting gold coins by 75 BC and establishing themselves in east Hampshire, Berkshire and Sussex. North of the river Thames the Catuvellauni and Trinovantes extended from south Bedfordshire to Essex and were striking coins by 60 BC, as were the Iceni in Norfolk. For the next century much of the history of southern Britain is the story of the feuds between these two rival factions and their attempts to dominate the indigenous peripheral tribes to the north and west.

The tribes of the south-east each introduced a series of gold, silver and bronze coins and attempted to imitate the Romans by writing the names of their chieftains on them in capital letters. On one side of the coin they sometimes displayed an ear of barley. This may have symbolised British nationalism – the barley from which they brewed their native beer, as opposed to the imported wines, symbolised by the vine leaf, which appeared on the coins of the supporters of Rome. The oldest inscribed British coins were struck for Commius, a Gallo-Belgic leader who fled to Britain and became chief of the Atrebates around 45 BC. Coins inscribed with the names of his three putative sons, Tincommius, Epillus and Verica, have also been found. North of the Thames inscribed Trinovantian coins of Addedomaros appeared about 40 BC, and the first joint Trinovantian and Catuvellaunian coins to bear a name were minted by Tasciovanus (25 BC to AD 10). They also bore the legend RIGNON ('high king') and the letters VER or CAM indicating their place of minting: Verulamium or Camulodunum. His son Cunobelinus reigned from AD 10 to 41, bringing stability and prosperity to his kingdom.

A large number of iron sword- and spit-shaped bars with flanged ends have been found in western hillforts and rivers from the Cotswolds to the Humber. Since many of them were hoarded and presumably of value, they are best identified as **currency bars**, mentioned by Caesar as a medium of barter, especially in territories north and west of the coin-using tribes.

With the growth of tribal kingdoms in south-east England during the first century BC a certain amount of centralised planning seems to have taken place. The number of hillforts was rationalised. A great many passed out of use. A few like Bigbury and Oldbury in Kent were retained and even strengthened, as tribal meeting places and headquarters. They became part of an heterogeneous group known by archaeologists as **enclosed oppida**. These were often located on low-lying ground close to river crossings. Their defences were a combination of earthworks and the river itself. Dyke Hills at Dorchester (Oxfordshire) encloses 46 hectares, and aerial photographs show that it was filled with a disorderly scatter of hundreds of circular huts. Salmonsbury, a 23 hectare site at Bourton-on-the-Water (Gloucestershire), utilised the river Windrush and marshes on two sides for protection. Similar sites are known at Loose in Kent and Winchester (Hampshire). All that have been excavated are of first-century BC date. Some of these sites continued to be occupied into Roman times, whilst others were abandoned in favour of new 'open' settlements close by. The new open sites were urban centres and are referred to as **territorial oppida**. In some cases they seem to have sprawled into the countryside with no clear boundaries, as at Canterbury or Verulamium. Others developed within territorial areas that were clearly delineated by massive linear dykes, though these might be placed some kilometres from the settlements themselves. Good examples include Camulodunum (Colchester, Essex), Silchester (Hampshire), Chichester (West Sussex) and Bagendon (Gloucestershire). These oppida seem, by our standards, to have been squalid but effective markets where it was possible to buy a wide range of fine goods,

62. Native late iron age wheel-turned pottery such as this would have been available throughout most of southern Britain.

some imported from the Roman world, and others of native manufacture (figure 62). These included vessels and mirrors of bronze, high-quality table wares including wine jugs and tankards, everyday kitchen equipment, luxurious jewellery and amphorae full of Mediterranean wines and sauces.

In the remoter parts of Britain the inhabitants continued to live in, or close to, hillforts, some of which were enlarged and strengthened as rumours of Roman troop movements increased. Stanwick in North Yorkshire is the only hillfort in northern England that might be seen as a territorial oppidum. It is a vast site of some 290 hectares, situated at the heart of Brigantian territory. Although it had only a small settlement area it utilised fine-quality pottery and metalwork (figure 63).

A group of iron age people at Glastonbury in Somerset built an artificial island in a lake (now dried out), on which a village of eighty timber houses was eventually built. There were never more than half a dozen houses standing at one time. The larger buildings were strongly made of carefully carpentered wood. They had clay floors and central hearths that gradually sank into the lake bed, necessitating the need to rebuild them frequently. The occupants used fine pottery decorated with curving Celtic patterns, probably manufactured in the Mendips nearby, and many wooden lathe-turned vessels which have survived in the waterlogged marshes.

63. Stanwick in North Yorkshire is likely to have been a vast tribal oppidum. A small part of the rock-cut defensive ditch and wall have been exposed.

Large numbers of bone combs were found for use in weaving, but no textiles were preserved. Close by, at Meare, two settlements on the edge of a raised bog contained much flimsier huts. John Coles has suggested that they were used for some kind of annual 'trade fair' where goods were exchanged and a variety of social activities took place.

During the second and first centuries BC, from far away in the Mediterranean, Rome was expanding its empire, and its influence was being felt throughout Europe. Roman traders were making their way ever northwards, infiltrating the barbarian tribes and introducing them to the intoxicating pleasures of wine in return for metal ores, hides, furs and slaves. Thick pottery wine containers (amphorae) of the early first century BC have been found in large numbers along the south-west coast of Brittany, in Guernsey and around Poole Harbour in Dorset, where Hengistbury Head seems to have been the major entrepot. Not only wine but vessels of coloured glass, Breton pottery and even figs were imported, and metal ores, grain, salt, cattle and possibly slaves and dogs were sent back to Brittany.

It became normal in the first century BC in south-east England to cremate the dead, placing the ashes in urns or bronze buckets, and burying them in cemeteries of flat graves. These often also contained distinctive wheel-made pottery types including tall pear-

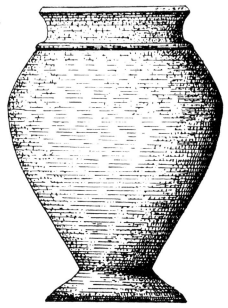

64. A wheel-turned Belgic cremation urn, 45 cm high.

shaped urns (figure 64). The burials were sometimes arranged in circles suggesting family groups. In an extensive cemetery excavated near Prae Wood at St Albans (Hertfordshire) 463 individual cremations were unearthed. Many of them had been placed in urns buried in small pits, together with such personal items as brooches, bronze mirrors and keys. Shallow ditches separating groups of burials suggest that the cemetery was divided into ancestral plots.

There are almost a dozen extremely rich graves from the Catuvellaunian area of Essex, Hertfordshire, Bedfordshire and Cambridgeshire, which may have belonged to chieftains or their ladies. These **Welwyn-type burials**, named after one of the find spots, consist of cremations placed in large rectangular graves without covering mounds, and accompanied by rich grave goods, including imported metal and glass, and amphorae which would have held many pints of wine. The Lexden tumulus, a kingly barrow still visible in Fitzwalter Road, Colchester, was excavated in 1924. The burial and contents had all been deliberately broken and burnt, but it was possible to recognise parts of a great iron chest, chain mail, some kind of robe made of solid gold threads and decorated with golden wheat ears, a quantity of fine bronzes, as well as the inevitable wine jars. These were the funeral accompaniments of a great prince, and it is possible that the grave, dated to between 15 and 10 BC, may have been that of Tasciovanus, king of the Trinovantes. Two other comparably rich burials have been excavated in Colchester and at Folly Lane, St Albans; but both are some sixty years later in date.

The Celts, like the other prehistoric peoples before them, worshipped a rich variety of deities, including horned nature gods and tribal warrior gods. Religious observance dominated their lives and signs of its power would have been all about them. Their shrines seem to have been natural open-air features such as the sources of rivers, streams and wells, all with healing powers, or groves of trees, single trees, unusual rocks, bogs, pools and islands. In a number of cases actual temple foundations have been identified: rectangular in shape at Heathrow (Surrey) and South Cadbury (Somerset), and circular at Maiden Castle (Dorset) and Hayling Island (Hampshire). Of the **Druids**, the officials who implemented the religion, we know little, although a vast amount of spurious literature has grown up around them. We are told that they were recruited from the warrior aristocracy, and that it was their function to intercede with a god or goddess on behalf of the people. Young men trained for twenty years in order to join the priesthood. According to Caesar the doctrine of the Druids was that 'souls do not suffer death, but after death pass from one body to another'. The most abhorrent side of druidism was the apparent need to please the barbarous gods with human sacrifice and the casting of gifts, including human beings, into sacred pools and marshes. The foretelling of the future from twitching human entrails was also required (figure 65).

From time to time well-preserved human bodies have been found in British marshes and peat deposits. It is only recently that their great antiquity has been recognised. It seems likely that some may have been druidical sacrifices. In 1984 the greater part of the body of a young man was found in a peat bog at Lindow in Cheshire. He had been struck on the head, garotted and had his throat cut. His body had been decorated with blue paint. The corpse, which is now in the British Museum, has been dated to the first century AD. The remains of at least two other people have been found at the same site.

The power of the Druids seems to have increased in the years immediately before the Roman occupation, and we learn of 'schools' of druidism in Britain. With the arrival of the Romans the Druids were forced into Wales and ultimately destroyed by the Roman commander Suetonius Paulinus in his attack on Anglesey in AD 60.

With the coming of the Romans, too, Celtic nationalism seems to have been rapidly driven underground in England, although it persisted in the remoter parts of Wales and Scotland and flourished in Ireland, which was never subjected to Roman rule.

In 55 and 54 BC **Julius Caesar** carried out two reconnaissance raids on south-eastern England in which his main objective seems to have been the subjection of the Catuvellauni and a number of small Belgic tribes north of the Thames. We are told that he attacked the tribal stronghold of Cassivellaunus, their overall leader, who escaped but was eventually forced to sue for peace. The stronghold was probably in Catuvellaunian territory, perhaps in Hertfordshire. Caesar left Britain after levying a tribute, which seems unlikely to have been paid for very long. In the years that followed his visits a series of inter-dynastic struggles raged in England. The Atrebates and Regnii supported diplomatic allegiance to Rome, whilst the Catuvellauni remained staunchly independent. After the death of Cassivellaunus he was succeeded by various chieftains, until about 25 BC coins of Tasciovanus appear, marked VER and minted at Prae Wood near pre-Roman Verulamium (St Albans, Hertfordshire). His territory spanned the Chilterns and Essex, and for a brief period his capital was at Camulodunum (Colchester). Tasciovanus' son, **Cunobelinus**, reigned for more than thirty years from AD 10, and established Camulodunum as the capital of his extended Catuvellaunian empire, which by then stretched from Northamptonshire to the Kentish coast, though it did not cover the territory of the Iceni who lived in Norfolk. So powerful was Cunobelinus that the Romans

65. Metal fittings from iron age chariots were recovered from a peat bog at Llyn Cerrig Bach in Anglesey in 1943.

66. The main iron age tribes of England and Wales on the eve of the Roman conquest.

referred to him as *Britannorum rex* (king of the Britons) (figure 66).

The greatest tribe in northern England, the Brigantes, was formed from a confederacy of small clans. It has been suggested that their great stronghold of 290 hectares at Stanwick (North Yorkshire) fell to the Romans soon after AD 72, although this is now open to question.

In Wales and northern England bronze age descendants continued to live in small farming communities, eking out a precarious living. Embanked enclosures containing small single or paired huts, with a paddock close by, were a common feature of the Pennine dales. Here, too, were nucleated villages like one identified at Grassington in Wharfedale with circular and oval stone huts some 15 to 30 metres across, clustered amongst 33 hectares of small rectangular fields. There were also the hillforts, often sited on prominent and impregnable mountain ridges. One of the finest in Wales is Tre'r Ceiri (Gwynedd), which existed as a native town throughout the Roman occupation. Inside its upstanding stone walls some 150 circular huts can still be seen. In Yorkshire and Northumbria smaller hilltop fortifications also continued into the Roman period. Although some of them, like Ingleborough (North Yorkshire), were slighted, others survived, even to continue in occupation after the Romans had left Britain.

THE ROMAN OCCUPATION
(AD 43 to 442)

In AD 43 the Emperor **Claudius**, anxious to establish himself as a great military leader, ordered the invasion of Britain by four legions and auxiliary troops totalling some forty thousand men, whilst a fifth legion remained in reserve. The general in command was Aulus Plautius. A rapid advance inland from Richborough (Kent) was followed by a decisive battle on the Medway near Rochester. The Thames was crossed near Westminster and the troops moved towards Camulodunum. A halt was then called so that Claudius could be present in person. In August AD 43, accompanied by part of the Praetorian Guard (the Emperor's personal bodyguard) and some elephants, he rode in state into the town, leaving again after sixteen days, his conquest completed!

The subjection of the west followed next, and by AD 47 most of lowland Britain south-east of the Fosse Way was occupied. In the next thirteen years the Romans spread into south-west England, south-east Wales and the Welsh Marches. A temporary setback occurred in AD 60 during a campaign against the Druids in Anglesey, when the **Iceni** of East Anglia rebelled under their queen, Boudicca, and destroyed the new Roman towns of Colchester, Verulamium and London. After Roman punitive action, a long period of consolidation followed. The Flavian advances of AD 74 led to the annexation of Wales and large parts of northern England. In AD 84, under Agricola, their limit was reached at the battle of Mons Graupius, somewhere to the east of Inverness. The occupation of Scotland was temporary and Hadrian established his famous frontier wall between the Tyne and the Solway in AD 122. Continued trouble from the Scottish tribes necessitated moving the frontier further north in the form of the Antonine Wall in AD 142, but its success was short-lived, and the troops soon reverted to the boundary of Hadrian's Wall. An abortive attempt by the governor, Clodius Albinus, to bid for the imperial throne in AD 196 resulted in his withdrawal of many troops from Britain. It was left to the Emperor Septimus Severus to restore order to the unrest which followed, and to launch a punitive expedition into Scotland. He died at York in AD 211.

For the next eighty years Britain enjoyed a period of peace and prosperity, until AD 286 when the usurper Carausius established himself as Emperor in Britain, only to be murdered by Allectus, before Constantius arrived from Rome and recaptured Britain in the autumn of 296. Troops were removed from Hadrian's Wall, which led to barbarian incursions into northern England. From the middle of the third century marauding bands of sea-borne Saxon and Irish pirates began to loot the sea coasts. Consequently the Romans found it necessary to set up a series of forts along the south and east coasts in an effort to check the invaders. These were the forts of the **Saxon shore**.

In 367 a concerted attack was made on the province by Picts (from Scotland), Scots (from Ireland), Saxons (from the Low Countries) and Attacotti (from Ireland or the Western Isles), all at one fell stroke. The Romans were unprepared, their military establishments undermanned. Hadrian's Wall was attacked from the rear and overrun. The invaders roamed over northern England looting and burning, and supported by hundreds of army deserters, whilst slaves took advantage of the disorganisation to flee from their masters and add to the plundering in the south. It was two years before Count Theodosius was able to restore order and a great programme of repairs set in motion. Hadrian's Wall was once more restored, only to have its troops again reduced in 383 when Magnus Maximus made a bid for the imperial throne. This was the beginning of a series of troop withdrawals by imperial contenders, which steadily drained Britain of its military strength. By 410 there were no legions left in Britain and the Emperor Honorius gave the British cities permission to defend themselves. This they endeavoured to do in the face of continuing attacks from the Picts and Saxons. Leaders like Vortigern were elected to organise the defence of the country. By the beginning of his 'reign' (AD 425) the Picts were regarded as the major enemy, and we are told that he was responsible for inviting Saxon mercenaries into Kent about 430 to help defend it. At first the arrangement was successful but in 442 the Saxons rebelled and 'Britain passed under the authority of the Saxons'.

Administration

With the Roman conquest much of Britain entered the Classical world, which had a somewhat more advanced technology than its own, and an elaborate financial and economic structure that had a profound effect on trade and commerce. It was Rome's intention to see that all conquered territories became self-governing as soon as possible. To this end the tribes retained many responsibilities through their native leaders. A tribal council (*ordo*) was drawn from about one hundred wealthy native landowners. From it two pairs of magistrates were elected annually to run the everyday affairs of the administrative districts (*civitates*) into which Britain was divided. These districts, which combined town and country, corresponded fairly closely to the late iron age tribal divisions. The *ordo* was ultimately responsible to the Roman governor and the procurator, who primarily dealt with judicial and financial matters respectively.

Roman towns

There were at least three reasons for the foundation of towns in Roman Britain. The **coloniae** were deliberate government settlements of veteran Roman soldiers. Colchester, Lincoln and Gloucester are good examples. Outside Roman forts and posting stations trading settlements (**vici**) grew up and often remained after the forts were abandoned. Such towns include Water Newton and Exeter. A third type of town was founded as a successor to an iron age centre, either on the site of or close to the earlier settlement

67. The Roman theatre at Verulamium (St Albans, Hertfordshire). The pillar (reconstructed) marks the front of the inner stage. The audience sat on wooden seats covering the low banks on the left.

68. The Fosse Way, a Roman road, about 16 km south of Warwick. Separating the parishes of Wellesbourne (left) and Combrook (right) in the foreground, the road runs north-east towards Ratae (Leicester).

(**civitas capitals**). Leicester and Silchester belong to this class.

In many cases the Roman towns lie buried under modern cities or villages, and little remains to be seen on the surface. A few are in the open countryside, but cost of upkeep prevents any extensive areas from being uncovered for permanent public inspection. Parts of Roman city walls, mostly built between AD 230 and 280, exist in a number of towns, including Verulamium, Silchester, Colchester, London, Wroxeter, York and Caerwent. Gateways can be seen at Lincoln and Colchester, whilst traces of internal buildings well worth a visit include the temple, market place and town hall at Caerwent, the public baths at Bath, the town hall at Wroxeter and the theatre and houses at Verulamium (figure 67). At Dover it is possible to see a town house with walls painted in bright colours, still standing over 1.8 metres high. Amphitheatres survive at Cirencester, Chester, Caerleon and Dorchester (Dorset).

Roman roads

The Romans constructed more than six thousand miles of roads in Britain, and many of them still underlie present-day main roads (figure 68). The earliest roads were built by the legions to cover the greatest distances as directly as possible, in order that troops might be moved quickly from one danger point to another. For this reason they tended to be straight, and it is often easy to follow their route on modern Ordnance Survey maps. The course of some roads changed as the requirements of traffic altered, and many minor roads appeared connecting towns to villas and industrial centres.

69. A mosaic showing a leopard and other exotic animals from the Roman villa at Woodchester (Gloucestershire).

The most obvious feature of a Roman road is the embankment forming the metalling, which was known as the **agger**. On main roads the agger varied between 9 and 15 metres in width and between 10 and 60 cm in thickness. Side ditches were often dug, especially when the road was passing through farmland. They tended to mark a zone within which the road was built rather than acting as drainage ditches. The ditches were separated from the agger by a flat space (**berm**) 3 to 7.5 metres in width. An excellent example of the features of a Roman road can be seen in the Stane Street as it runs across the South Downs, not far from the villa at Bignor near Chichester in West Sussex.

The Roman countryside

More prosperous iron age farmers who continued to trade in Roman Britain could afford to replace their wooden huts with farmhouses in the Roman style. These new farms (called **villas**) began as suites of rooms on a rectangular plan connected along one side by a corridor or verandah. As time went by and prosperity increased such villas were enlarged by adding wings at each end of the main building, which might contain luxury rooms with mosaic floors and bath blocks (figure 69). However, the majority of villas had neither mosaics nor baths. Many of the villas were of half-timber construction on stone wall bases. From the villa the farmer controlled large estates either as owner or sometimes as a tenant for the government. Occasionally rich Roman officials might buy villas as country retreats. They would employ a number of tenant farmers and slaves (some of whom still lived in round huts) to manage parts of the estate for them. Sheep farming and corn growing were of considerable importance, whilst market gardening, fruit production and vine cultivation were frequently practised. A few villas seem to have been the centres of local industries like mining, quarrying and pottery making, and in those cases agriculture seems to have been of minor importance, if it existed at all.

Villas such as Lullingstone (Kent), Chedworth (Gloucestershire), Bignor (West Sussex) and Brading (Isle of Wight) well repay careful study. Continuity from a late iron age farmstead to a stone-built villa is clearly demonstrated at the Bancroft villa in Milton Keynes (Buckinghamshire). The palace at Fishbourne (West Sussex), probably built by the Romans for Cogidubnus, the native ruler of the Regnenses who had found favour with the conquerors, is one of the more interesting Roman buildings in southern England.

Most of the native population continued to live in iron age villages all over Britain. These were collections of huts often linked by trackways to Roman roads and towns. In the West Country courtyard houses, like the group at Chysauster (Cornwall), are a late iron age survival that flourished into the first and second centuries AD. Many hillforts had been slighted at the onset of the invasion (Maiden Castle and Hod Hill, Dorset) and, whilst there is evidence that some natives continued to occupy them, others moved to lower undefended sites. Apart from labouring on farms, the native Britons worked as carpenters, builders, brickmakers, metalworkers, weavers, potters, miners, as well as a host of other trades. Romanisation was particularly strong in the towns and the countryside immediately around them, as well as in the military areas. The natives were romanised to the extent of using Roman coins, pottery and metal goods, wearing Roman fashions and enjoying Roman foods and drink. Their native gods were usually romanised in inscriptions, and Latin graffiti was not uncommon. Consequently they are often referred to as **Romano-Britons**.

Supplementing the network of roads all over southern Britain, navigable rivers allowed goods to be transported by boats of shallow draft to inland towns like York, Lincoln and even Wroxeter. At least one canal, the Foss Dyke, is known. It connected the rivers Witham and Trent. In the West Country and elsewhere metal ores and minerals were being mined soon after the Roman conquest: lead and silver from the Mendips and Derbyshire, iron from the Forest of Dean and Weald of Kent, copper from Anglesey, tin from Cornwall and in many places coal and building stone. Ports along the east coast allowed for the import of luxury goods such as the fine orange table pottery called **samian** from Gaul, glass and bronzes from the Rhineland, wine and oil from Spain and textiles and ornaments from the Mediterranean.

Religion and death

Once druidism had been stamped out, the only religious demand the Romans made on the native Britons was the observance of their official religion centred on the Capitoline Triad (Jupiter, Juno and Minerva) and the deified Emperor. Provided this was respected, they were free to worship any other local gods that they chose. Temples to the Persian god **Mithras** in London, Colchester and on Hadrian's Wall exemplify this freedom. A large temple to the native god Nodens exists at Lydney (Gloucestershire), whilst 3 metres below the Pump Room at Bath and under the castle at Colchester are the remains of temples built in the classical style, dedicated to Sulis Minerva and the imperial cult respectively. On West Hill, Uley (Gloucestershire), an extensive temple complex dedicated to Mercury grew up on the site of an earlier iron age shrine and close to a neolithic long barrow. A number of tiny Romano-Celtic temples, consisting of a square building (*cella*) surrounded by a verandah, have been found. Quite often they are on the tops of hills, as at Chanctonbury Ring (West Sussex) and Maiden Castle (Dorset) (figure 70).

70. The footings of a small Roman temple built after AD 367 inside the hillfort of Maiden Castle (Dorset).

Under Constantine the Great in AD 313 **Christian worship** was permitted. It became the official religion of the Roman empire in AD 391. There is little archaeological evidence for Christianity in Britain. A small church has been identified at Silchester, as has an aisled building at Verulamium (neither visible). Villas at Lullingstone (Kent) and Hinton St Mary (Dorset) contained rooms which were probably Christian chapels. A fourth-century mosaic from the Hinton St Mary villa, now in the British Museum, depicts a male head which may represent Christ together with the chi-rho symbol and pomegranates.

Roman burials

In the first and second centuries AD the Romans cremated their dead, placing the ashes in pottery urns or metal and wooden caskets. Inhumation burials, in a variety of wood, lead or stone coffins, were usual in the third and fourth centuries. There was a brief overlap between the two customs. Both types of burial were normally interred in flat cemeteries outside Roman settlements. Barrows commemorating the more illustrious dead often line Roman roadsides. They are often conical in shape with flat tops and can be quite large. One of the (originally) eight Bartlow Hills in Essex is 12 metres high and 44 metres in diameter. The Six Hills beside the London Road in the centre of Stevenage (Hertfordshire) and the barrows at Thornborough near Buckingham may be considered typical groups. It is noticeable that Roman barrows occur in the non-military south-eastern part of Britain and are often on low-lying ground, sometimes near water, which distinguishes them from the majority of surviving prehistoric barrows on higher ground.

Roman military sites

Earthwork enclosures, usually with straight sides and rounded corners, were a feature of all Roman military engineering. This makes it difficult to confuse Roman monuments with prehistoric ones. The main types of military sites constructed in Britain were:

1. Legionary fortresses. These were permanent military bases, varying in size from about 20 to 25 hectares. Rectangular in plan with four gates, they had corner towers on the straight sides, at intervals of 100 Roman feet, and external ditches. Most legionary forts underlie modern cities as at York and Chester, where traces of the walls can be seen. The best excavated example is at Caerleon in Gwent, a site which occupies about 20 hectares on a bend in the river Usk.

2. Smaller forts. All less than 4 hectares in extent, these were permanent bases for auxiliary troops and were planned on the same

71. The massive walls and bastions of Portchester (Hampshire), together with the defensive ditch on the right, are all of Roman workmanship.

lines as the legionary fortresses. They are found all over the north of England and Wales but only a few can still be seen. Of these the superbly sited Hardknott (Cumbria) and Segontium (Caernarfon) will repay a visit. The Saxon Shore forts of the late third and fourth centuries are fundamentally different, with a lack of internal buildings. The best-preserved is Portchester (Hampshire) (figure 71), with others at Pevensey (East Sussex) and Richborough (Kent). Near Coventry a cavalry base called The Lunt has been excavated and partially rebuilt with a gateway, a wooden stockade and a granary which forms a site museum. It is unusual in having a *gyrus*, or training ring for cavalry horses.

3. Fortlets and signal stations. Again concentrated in the military zone of Britain and along the coast, the fortlets provided small supply depots, whilst the signal stations rapidly relayed messages between the frontier and the main forts.

4. Temporary camps. These were usually constructed whilst the legions were campaigning in the north and west. Single rectangular banked enclosures varied in size from 1.2 to 40 hectares.

5. Hadrian's Wall. This, the most famous structure in Roman Britain, ran for 117 km from Wallsend-on-Tyne to Bowness-on-

72. Hadrian's Wall at Hotbank. It follows the crest of Steel Rigg Crags and Winshields Crags diagonally across the picture.

Solway (figure 72). Its eastern sector was built of stone 6 metres high and 3 metres thick. West of the river Irthing it was built of turf 3.6 metres high and 6 metres thick. This part was later rebuilt in stone. At every Roman mile (1482 metres) there was a milecastle for the patrolling garrison, and between each milecastle and the next there were two small turrets for sentries. On the northern side of the Wall ran a ditch, whilst to the south of it ran a banked and ditched earthwork called the *vallum* and a military road. These last two features postdate the sixteen forts which were built to house large garrisons of soldiers. Of these forts Birdoswald, Housesteads, Chesters (figure 73), Wallsend and South Shields are well worth visiting, as are Vindolanda, 1.6 km to the south of the Wall, and the supply base at Corbridge. At its strongest the total complement of defenders on Hadrian's Wall would have been about 9500 men.

POST-ROMAN BRITAIN
(AD 442 to 1066)

Life in Roman towns and villas continued into the middle of the fifth century, then rapidly broke down through lack of trade and finance, and at the hands of marauding bands of Picts and Saxons. Many people had moved into the security of the walled cities, and the find of a corn-drying oven dug through a mosaic at Verulamium indicates that it was considered safer to bring the harvest into the

112

city for storage. Many villas were reduced in size, and some left to the care of tenant farmers whilst their owners retired to the protection of the communal town life. The Latin language was abandoned in favour of British (except where the Christian church survived).

There was no organised Saxon invasion of Britain. Some Saxons had been invited into the country as mercenaries by Vortigern; others arrived in small groups determined to win land for themselves, whilst further groups had settled as traders and merchants in earlier Roman days. The scale of the Saxon settlements is still a matter of dispute. According to Bede, writing in 731, the immigrants had come 'from the three most powerful races of Germany: the Saxons, the Angles and the Jutes'. The Jutes claimed kingdoms in Kent and the Isle of Wight; the East, South and West Saxons in Essex, Sussex and Wessex; and the Angles in East Anglia and most of middle and eastern England from Gloucestershire to Northumberland. These claims are borne out by appropriate archaeological finds. Slowly the immigrants and the natives intermingled. That their presence was accepted in Britain is shown by Saxon cremations in Roman cemeteries at York. In some places their power was stronger than in others and in Kent and Yorkshire (Deira) they

73. The strongroom at Chesters fort on Hadrian's Wall. It had an oak-studded door which fell to pieces on excavation.

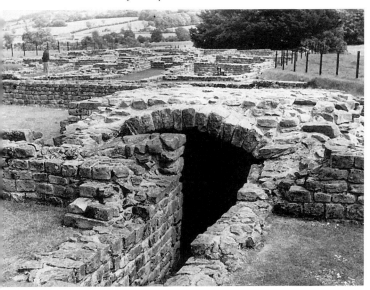

established their own kingdoms. As their strength increased so they eventually turned on the native British, who rallied and fought under their leaders Ambrosius Aurelianus and his successor Arthur. Finally the Saxons were defeated at Mount Badon (somewhere in the south-west), a little before AD 500. Fifty years of peace were followed by renewed Saxon conquests after 550, which slowly spread across Britain, until a serious defeat of the northern Britons at Catterick about 590 reduced the whole country, with the exception of the south-west and Wales, to a series of Saxon kingdoms. In Ireland and western Britain Celtic culture was preserved, to be reintroduced into the English kingdoms in the eighth century.

Saxon England developed as a number of independent states, of which the chief were Northumbria, Mercia, Wessex and East Anglia. The history of the sixth to eight centuries is the story of the interplay between these **Anglo-Saxon** kingdoms, and their relations with Ireland, Wales and Cornwall. The term Anglo-Saxon has long been used to distinguish the Saxons who lived in England from those who continued to live on the continent.

The Roman Christian church had collapsed in most parts of England by the early fifth century, although it seems to have survived in small cells in the south-west, the north-west and in Wales. Celtic **Christianity** spread from those western areas into Scotland soon after 500. By the middle of the seventh century Christianity had been restored to England by missions from the Celtic church in the north and St Augustine in the south. From then on many monasteries and churches were established, mainly in the south and east.

In 793 **Vikings** from Norway attacked the great monastery of Lindisfarne. After that, their piratical raids became more and more frequent on the north and west coasts. After 834 Danish Vikings began to raid the east coast. By 865 the first Viking settlements began to appear in eastern England and within a few years they established a kingdom for themselves with a capital at York (*Jorvik*). Excavations at Coppergate in York revealed the waterlogged remains of houses and workshops containing jewellery and cooking pots, tools and leather shoes. The site has been skilfully reconstructed and is one of the more spectacular archaeological features of the city.

Most of England was overrun by these Danish Vikings (**Danes**), before Alfred the Saxon managed to win back the south and Midlands, although in 886 he had to accept a division of the country, in which the Danes retained the area north and east of Watling Street and the river Lea. This area became known as the **Danelaw**. Alfred's son, Edward the Elder, united the kingdoms of Wessex and Mercia and brought all the Danish settlements south of the Humber under the rule of Wessex. He built a series of forts along the Danelaw boundary, traces of which still survive today.

A second series of Danish raids on England began soon after Aethelred's succession in 979, and in 991 a formidable Danish army attacked East Anglia. Peace was dearly bought by levying a heavy tax called Danegeld. Aethelred was driven from the country in 1014 by Sweyn of Denmark, but the latter's sudden death enabled Aethelred and his son Edmund Ironside to return. In 1016 Sweyn's son Cnut (Canute) became king of England, Denmark, Sweden and Norway. During his reign, and converted to Christianity, he built churches and monasteries. He also drained part of the Fens, built bridges, developed a strong merchant navy and established excellent trade relations with much of northern Europe. His two short-lived sons in turn succeeded him on his death in 1035, and in 1042 Edward (the Confessor), son of Edmund Ironside, was chosen king.

Although the Saxons were initially rural people, by the ninth century many had adjusted to the idea of living in towns. This was partly in response to the need for protection against the Danish raids, and partly to facilitate trade. Some towns, such as Northampton and Tamworth (Staffordshire), were **royal centres**. Others on the south and east coasts were trading towns (*wics*), Ipswich and Hamwic (Southampton) being proven by excavation. At the latter the remains of more than sixty-five houses with wattle and daub walls and thatched roofs, together with sheds, wells, pits, cemeteries and a tiny church have been uncovered.

A number of villages with smaller domestic dwellings have been examined in recent years. One of the largest and earliest, at Mucking in Essex, produced the postholes of some fifty halls and 210 *Grubenhäuser* – small, single-roomed huts with floors sunk half a metre below the ground surface. At West Stow (Suffolk) a hamlet of four farms, each comprising halls and sunken buildings, was rebuilt several times. Part of it has been reconstructed on the original site. Royal palaces at Yeavering (Northumberland) and Cheddar (Somerset) have been unearthed, displaying extensive complexes of wooden halls and outbuildings of the ninth to eleventh centuries.

A number of iron age hillforts were refortified in Saxon times and occupied at later dates. At South Cadbury (Somerset) the ancient fort had new defences built in the fifth and sixth centuries AD; it contained a great wooden hall, more than 18 metres long. Abandoned after 577, it was refortified and occupied between 1010 and 1017 by Aethelred II. Bow-sided boat-shaped wooden houses of the later Saxon period are known from Maxey, Eaton Socon and Buckden (all in Cambridgeshire) and Long Wittenham

(Oxfordshire), although none are now visible.

The best indications that Saxon settlements once existed are the strip lynchets and cemeteries that have been found nearby. **Strip lynchets** are usually found on the scarp faces of chalk downland and represent the contour ploughing of the Saxons, though some can be documented to the early medieval period. After ploughing, the soil on the hillslope tended to slide and creep downhill and to pile up in terraces wherever it met an obstruction such as a fence, wall or other field boundary. The absence of 'Celtic' fields in the Chilterns has led to the suggestion that some strip lynchets in eastern England, often close to hillforts, may be of iron age origin.

Remains of the early Saxons in Britain are to be seen mainly in museums, where the weapons and jewellery excavated from their cemeteries are displayed. Yet this is only part of the evidence. A detailed study of their skeletal remains gives us vital information about their age, health, nutrition and even blood grouping, as well as occasional dramatic details of the way in which they died.

Many of the earliest pagan Saxons cremated their dead, placing the ashes in bulbous-looking urns (figure 74). Others chose inhumation and corpses were placed in large **cemeteries** of flat graves accompanied by ornaments and weapons. There seems to have been complete freedom of choice and both types of burial practice are found together.

74. Hand-made Saxon cremation urns decorated with oval bosses and stamped patterns.

Saxon **barrows** are found in various parts of southern and eastern England, with outliers in the Yorkshire Wolds and Peak District. They seem to cover the graves of the richer members of society. The burial of a woman beneath a round barrow on Roundway Down (Wiltshire) was accompanied by a luxurious necklace composed of four gold metal beads and seven garnet cabochon gold pendants, together with a gold and garnet pin-suite. Some barrow burials lay on wooden beds, as at Barrington (Cambridgeshire) and Swallowcliffe Down (Wiltshire). Under a great barrow overlooking the Thames at Taplow old churchyard (Buckinghamshire) lay a prince in gold-embroidered clothing, accompanied by a sword, three shields and an armoury of spears. His grave also contained a wooden tub, a metal-framed bucket, a bronze bowl, pottery, glass beakers, drinking horns, personal jewellery and a set of draughtsmen.

More princely barrow cemeteries have been excavated at Snape and Sutton Hoo (Suffolk). At both sites boat burials have been found. The most famous was in Mound I at **Sutton Hoo**, where the impression of a clinker-built wooden rowing-boat 27 metres long was uncovered in 1939. At its centre a wooden burial chamber was found containing many fragments of the helmet, chain mail, shield and weapons of a warrior, much of it of gold, richly decorated with garnets. Such a wealthy burial points to the grave of a king (though the acid soil had destroyed all trace of the body). It is generally assumed that this was King Raedwald of East Anglia, who died about 624. Further excavation in the 1960s examined six more barrows at Sutton Hoo, one of which contained the robbed remains of a second, smaller boat. A series of flat graves was also uncovered, containing 'sandmen' (page 28). Grave goods ceased to be buried with the dead after the end of the seventh century, following the conversion to Christianity.

The religious architecture of Saxon England must now be considered. Nothing is known of pagan sanctuaries, although it is believed that one of the smaller wooden halls at Yeavering may have formed a Christian chapel.

There is no evidence that Roman Christianity survived in southeastern Britain through the pagan Saxon period, although many Christian churches still stood in ruins when St Augustine came to Britain in 597. Many of the early **churches** were built of wood, and one has survived in part at Greenstead-juxta-Ongar in Essex. They were often defended with a bank and ditch or drystone wall, or existing secular defences were taken over, as at the mid-Saxon monastery of St Fursey in Burgh Castle (Norfolk), though no sign of it now remains to be seen. Many monasteries were destroyed by the Vikings but were partly rebuilt by the end of Alfred's reign.

The late Saxon cathedral at North Elmham (Norfolk) was built at the end of the tenth century.

Although the Roman circular apse was built in Saxon churches directly influenced by St Augustine, most wooden churches had square east ends, a feature which has survived to the present day. A fine seventh-century example with an apse can be seen at Brixworth (Northamptonshire), which incorporates reused Roman bricks.

75. The stripwork-decorated tower of Earls Barton church (Northamptonshire). The battlemented top course is a later addition.

76. The Saxon church of St Laurence at Bradford-on-Avon (Wiltshire).

Stone replaced wood for building in the eighth century. Ground plans were simple: a rectangular nave with narrow chancel arch and a western tower, and sometimes porches to north and south producing a cruciform effect. Features of the architecture include 'long and short' bonding at angles (horizontal stones alternating with vertical ones), 'turned' stone baluster-shaped shafts in windows, and round or triangular arches to doorways and windows (figure 75). One of the most perfect examples of a Saxon church in England is St Laurence's at Bradford-on-Avon in Wiltshire, which dates from the early tenth century, forming a link between the early pre-Viking building period and the revival at the time of Cnut (figure 76).

Close to the seashore in western England and Wales are some of the earliest Christian funeral monuments. These are the memorial stones inscribed in Latin or Irish recording the burial places of Christians of the fifth to seventh centuries. A few of them may have been set up by Irish missionaries. Some of the inscriptions are

77. Offa's Dyke, running south from Spoad Hill, 5 km to the west of Clun in Shropshire.

in ogam lettering; this was a non-alphabetical system of stroke writing used in Ireland and consisted of long and short lines and groups of lines standing for different letters. Good examples can be seen at Lewannick and St Clement in Cornwall and Caldey Island (Pembrokeshire).

There are few signs of early Saxon defensive works apart from linear boundary earthworks such as Wansdyke and Offa's Dyke (built around 780) (figure 77), and shorter dykes which close gaps in natural defences like forests, such as those in Cambridgeshire or Bokerley Dyke (Dorset) (figure 78). The latter was the culmination of a series of cultural boundaries originating in the bronze age. In the ninth century earthworks were constructed between the rivers Frome and Piddle at Wareham (Dorset), at Wallingford (Oxfordshire) and at Cricklade (Wiltshire), where the town is still enclosed by an earthwork 410 metres square. These are all **burhs** of the type ordered by King Alfred for the defence of Wessex.

If the semicircular enclosure called the King's Ditch on the south bank of the river Ouse at Bedford is the remains of Edward the Elder's burh, then there is reason to believe that he was basing his design on the Danish forts which had been built along the Danelaw frontier. These were often D-shaped enclosures with a river forming the straight side, and a stockade and ditch marking

78. The Devil's Dyke in Cambridgeshire is 12 km long. It was probably constructed early in the fifth century AD as a boundary between the Saxons and the British.

the curved enemy-facing bow. Such sites have been identified at Repton (Derbyshire) and tentatively at Beeston (now destroyed) and Shillington in Bedfordshire.

The arrival of the Normans in England towards the end of 1066 reinforced new ideas in architecture and fashion that had been reaching the country from Normandy for some time. It is with the imposition of this new culture on the English way of life, the last military invasion in England's history, that we bring this brief survey to a close.

It is up to the reader now to seek out the archaeological sites that have been described, to examine the evidence of our ancestors displayed in museums throughout Britain, and to obtain further information from the wealth of books written about those aspects of the subject which he or she finds of particular interest.

4
Taking part

If you would like to learn more about archaeology on a local or national level, then you might consider joining one of the many archaeological societies in Britain. Some of these are old-established and reliable county societies, often with their own museums and publishing annual journals, like the Wiltshire Archaeological and Natural History Society (founded in 1853), with many professional and experienced amateur members. In recent years a rash of new societies has appeared, often as a result of evening courses in archaeology. Some are very good, but others are of a more dubious nature, and it is as well to check their credentials before joining. Most of them hold monthly lectures in the winter and run excursions in the summer. If they excavate, ask to see their published reports, and if they cannot produce them go elsewhere!

The most seriously interested readers should consider joining one of the national archaeological societies, which also organise monthly lectures, annual conferences and British and foreign excursions and publish annual journals and other occasional publications. The most accessible are the Royal Archaeological Institute, c/o Society of Antiquaries, Burlington House, Piccadilly, London W1V 0HS; the Prehistoric Society and the Society for the Promotion of Roman Studies, both c/o University College London, Institute of Archaeology, 31-34 Gordon Square, London WC1H 0PY. Write to their respective secretaries for details.

Finding an excavation where volunteers are welcome has become difficult in recent years. In the 1960s and 1970s there were hundreds of digs needing helpers, and paying a subsistence allowance to the volunteers. Ironically today, with archaeology hijacked by professional units, it is common for untrained diggers from the Job Centre to be employed at great expense, to the detriment of knowledgeable trained but amateur workers, who are willing to give their services free. In many cases the organisers have the gall to expect volunteers to pay for the privilege of working for them! The Council for Independent Archaeology (CIA) runs an excavation placement service and endeavours to put would-be diggers in touch with suitable excavations. The CIA welcomes amateur members and details can be obtained from the Secretary, 3 West Street, Weedon Bec, Northampton NN7 4QU. The excavation placement service is organised by Kevan Fadden, 7 Lea Road, Ampthill, Bedford MK45 2PR. Please enclose stamped and addressed envelopes when writing for information.

Many local education authorities, university extra-mural departments and the Workers' Educational Association run courses on archaeology and related topics during the winter months. Some of these lead to diplomas and certificates in Archaeology. As a first step, the easiest way to get information about many of these is to consult the current edition of the highly informative (but very expensive) *British Archaeological Yearbook*, published by the Council for British Archaeology (CBA), Bowes Morrell House, 111 Walmgate, York YO1 2UA (telephone: 01904 671417). The CBA is a government-funded body promoting all aspects of archaeology in Britain. Individuals may take out annual membership. The fee includes copies of the magazine *British Archaeology*; there is a reduced rate for students. A free fact sheet (Number 8) on archaeological excavations is available on request. Children aged nine to sixteen can join the Young Archaeologists' Club, an archaeological organisation for young people with sixteen branches around Britain. For more information write to or telephone the Club, c/o the CBA at the York address above.

About 450 ancient monuments in England and Wales are cared for by English Heritage and Cadw (Welsh Historic Monuments). Both publish excellent guide books and organise special events and concerts. Readers will find it worthwhile to become members and make considerable savings on entrance costs. Apply to English Heritage Membership Department, PO Box 1BB, London W1A 1BB (telephone: 0171-973 3400). English Heritage also operates a useful education service for teachers, supplying advice, information packs, slides and videos. Contact English Heritage Education Service, 429 Oxford Street, London W1R 2HD (telephone: 0171-973 3442 or 3443). For information about Cadw membership and its education service contact Welsh Historic Monuments, Brunel House, 2 Fitzalan Road, Cardiff CF2 1UY (telephone: 01222 500200). Cadw publishes a series of excellent *Guides to Ancient and Historical Wales.*

Further reading

Methods, techniques and general works

Barker, P. *Techniques of Archaeological Excavation.* Batsford, 1993.

Brown, A. *Fieldwork for Archaeologists and Local Historians.* Batsford, 1987.

Greene, K. *Archaeology: An Introduction.* Batsford, 1995.

Renfrew, C., and Bahn, P. *Archaeology: Theories, Methods and Practice.* Thames & Hudson, 1996.

Wass, S. *The Amateur Archaeologist.* Batsford, 1992.

Wood, E.S. *Historical Britain.* Harvill, 1995.

Prehistory

Bewley, R. *Prehistoric Settlements.* Batsford, 1994.

Burl, A. *Prehistoric Avebury.* Yale, 1979.

Burl, A. *The Stonehenge People.* Dent, 1987.

Cunliffe, B. *Iron Age Britain.* Batsford, 1995.

Darvill, T. *Prehistoric Britain.* Batsford, 1995.

Dyer, J. *Ancient Britain.* Batsford, 1995.

Edmonds, M. *Stone Tools and Society.* Batsford, 1995.

James, S., and Rigby, V. *Britain and the Celtic Iron Age.* British Museum Press, 1997.

Parker-Pearson, M. *Bronze Age Britain.* Batsford, 1993.

Richards, J. *Stonehenge.* Batsford, 1991.

Sharples, N. *Maiden Castle.* Batsford, 1991.

Roman Britain

Frere, S.S. *Britannia: A History of Roman Britain.* Routledge, 1987.

Johnson, S. *Hadrian's Wall.* Batsford, 1989.

Jones, B., and Mattingly, D. *An Atlas of Roman Britain.* Blackwell, 1990.

Millett, M. *Roman Britain.* Batsford, 1995.

Ottaway, P. *Archaeology in British Towns.* Routledge, 1992.

Potter, T.W., and Johns, C. *Roman Britain.* British Museum Press, 1992.

Salway, P. *Oxford Illustrated History of Roman Britain.* Oxford University Press, 1993.

Post-Roman Britain

Evans, A.C. *The Sutton Hoo Ship Burial.* British Museum Press, 1994.

Hall, R. *Viking Age York.* Batsford, 1994.
Richards, J.D. *Viking Age England.* Batsford, 1991.
Thomas, C. *Celtic Britain.* Thames & Hudson, 1986.
Welch, M. *Anglo-Saxon England.* Batsford, 1992.

Guide books

Burl, A. *A Guide to the Stone Circles of Britain, Ireland and Brittany.* Yale, 1995.
Dyer, J. *Penguin Guide to Prehistoric England and Wales.* Penguin, 1982.
Dyer, J. *Discovering Prehistoric England.* Shire, 1993.
Ellis, P.B. *A Guide to Early Celtic Remains in Britain.* Constable, 1991.
Johnson, D.E. *Discovering Roman Britain.* Shire, 1993.
Laing, L. and J. *A Guide to the Dark Age Remains in Britain.* Constable, 1979.

Shire Archaeology

This comprehensive series of more than seventy titles covers most aspects of British archaeology. For a free catalogue write to Shire Publications Ltd, Cromwell House, Church Street, Princes Risborough, Buckinghamshire HP27 9AA.

Magazines

For the enthusiast who wishes to study the subject further the following magazines can be recommended:

Current Archaeology: published six times a year and available only on subscription from 9 Nassington Road, London NW3 2TX. Readers receive a most useful annual *Directory of British Archaeology* containing names and addresses of archaeological organisations.

British Archaeology: ten issues a year from the Council for British Archaeology, Bowes Morrell House, 111 Walmgate, York YO1 2UA. Members also receive *Briefing,* a supplement listing fieldwork, courses, events and books.

Heritage Today: the magazine of English Heritage, which sometimes contains articles of archaeological interest.

Index

Page numbers in italic refer to illustrations.